Stocks & Shares

A Daily Telegraph
Investor's Handbook

Stocks & Shares

Roger Hardman

Published by Telegraph Publications,
Peterborough Court, At South Quay,
181 Marsh Wall, London E14 9SR

© Telegraph Publications/William Curtis Ltd 1987

1st edition September 1986
1st reprint October 1986
2nd reprint December 1986
2nd edition September 1987

Typeset by Rowland Phototypesetting Ltd,
Bury St Edmunds, Suffolk
Printed in Great Britain by Biddles Ltd,
Guildford and King's Lynn

Series Editor: Marlene Garsia

British Library Cataloguing in Publication Data
Hardman, Roger
  Stocks and Shares. – 2nd ed.
  1. Investments – Great Britain 2. Stocks
  – Great Britain
  I. Title
  332.6'322   HG5432

  ISBN 0-86367-108-X
  ISBN 0-86367-173-X Pbk

R J THOMPSON & CO.

MEMBERS OF THE STOCK EXCHANGE

Q How do I choose a stockbroker?

A There are several questions you will want answered before making a selection. As a rule of thumb, you will ask in what type of client each firm specialises, when the company was established and what services it offers. You should check whether there is a minimum transaction size and if the firm sets a lower limit on the value of portfolios.

Q Why R J Thompson & Co?

A ■ Specialists in private client portfolios
■ Personal informed service
■ Competitive fees
■ In-house research
■ Free advice without obligation
■ Established, respected firm
■ Confidently

Q What service does R J Thompson & Co offer clients?

A We advise on British and overseas shares, units trusts and fixed interest securities. Advice on pensions, assurance and inheritance tax is also available. In addition, one of the firm's partners researches companies as well as producing share circulars at appropriate times. Naturally, we execute transactions quickly and at the best prices obtainable. For expatriate clients, or people who travel overseas for prolonged periods, R J Thompson & Co offers a discretionary and nominee service.

Q Who will I deal with at R J Thompson & Co?

A All private clients deal direct with one of the firm's partners and receive personal attention at a senior level. In contrast, many firms' clients rarely talk to senior managers unless their portfolios are very substantial. At R J Thompson & Co there is no second best.

Q Who do I contact?

A For a confidential discussion of your investment needs, please telephone

**Roy Thompson
Sir Charles McLeod Bt**

or

Antony Beale
on: 01-588 2790

R J Thompson & Co
1 Salisbury House
London Wall
London
EC2M 5RH

References
We are required under Stock Exchange rules to refer new clients to the Stock Exchange Members' Mutual Reference Society, a registered credit agency for Stock Exchange members dealing with the public.

Contents

Foreword   11

1 The wonderful world of shares   15

– The British Telecom boom   15
– Should you be buying shares?   23
– How much money do you need?   26

2 There are safer ways of investing   29

– National Savings   30
– Bank deposit accounts   33
– Building society accounts   33
– Roll-up funds   33
– Insurance policies   34
– Gold   35
– Unit trusts   37
– Personal Equity Plans   43
– Investment trusts   45

3 Fixed interest investments   51

– Gilt-edged securities   51
– The yield curve   56

4 How to go about trading   63

– How to choose a broker   64
– How to deal   75
– Big Bang – its effect on investors   77

5 So many markets to choose from   83

– The currency factor   86
– Going international – the easy way   87

–The disadvantages 89
–But what is it all going to cost? 90

6 The meat of the matter – how professionals
   analyse shares 95

–Reverse yield gap 100
–Number of shares 101
–The price/earnings ratio 106
–What influences profits? 109
–Tax 116

7 Analysis in more detail 117

–Source and application of funds 123
–Inventory control 124
–Receivables/payables control 126
–Rights issues 127
–Scrip issues 131

8 Drawing your own charts 133

–Using charts 133
–Identifying and analysing different chart patterns 141
–Technical analysis 149
–Ways of drawing charts 152

9 Every sector tells a different story 159

–Agencies 159
–Banks 160
–Breweries 162
–Contracting 163
–Engineering 164
–Insurance 164
–Minerals 166
–Retailing 169
–Textiles 170

10 Your portfolio strategy 171

–Points to consider when making up your portfolio 172
–Other points to watch 178
–Wishing you a profitable investment 179

Contents

Glossary of terms   181

Appendix I   188
Sources of information

Index   190

Foreword

Your grandparents may well have owned shares – but not your parents. The trend away from investing on the stock market has been reversed, helped by a decade of rising share prices and considerable publicity surrounding a number of new share issues. One in five adults are now shareholders, and the Government's personal equity plans will boost that still further. British Telecom played a part in widening share ownership, but that was only one of a number of Government shares sales, and some private issues have caught the public's imagination equally – whether it was Richard Branson of Virgin bringing his talents to the stock market, Thames TV, or TSB.

Not every share issue has worked for investors – or not immediately. Still less, not every share bought through the market rather than when the company's shares were floated, has been a guaranteed winner. The general rise in stock market prices over the years has ensured that not too many fingers have been burned seriously. This is not to say that playing the stock market is easy, or that there is not a lot to learn. Profitable shares can be picked with a pin in a rising market and the winners may more often than not offset the losers. As the investor becomes more interested, educated and experienced, he can ensure that more of his portfolio will show profits and that those gains can be maximised.

This is where a book like this can help. For many readers, even the initial step of buying a share – or selling one inherited from someone else – may be new. Other readers will find the book invaluable as it explains the complexities, such as using charts to identify investment patterns. The stock market allows investors to treat it just as seriously as they want: some people quite literally make a career out of it, while others are happy to sit on the same portfolio of shares for years.

There are some complexities that cannot be avoided. Even the inactive investor sitting on that portfolio of shares will find himself receiving a fairly constant correspondence. Some of it, such as the profit reports and accounts may require little action – though the investor has the right to vote on the re-election of directors and a host of other issues, as well as to attend company meetings. However, other communications do require action. With luck there will be a couple of dividend cheques a year, there may also be rights issues asking for more money and he may receive a takeover offer from another company. Such a bid may mean a welter of circulars, but an extra profit as the share price rises.

The investor has to keep an alert eye on his shares, even before watching their performance in the market, and trying to predict what factors could cause prices to rise or dividends to increase – or to identify which factors indicate the time to sell.

But those people becoming share investors now are coming into the stock market at a time of change. Much of the mystique of share dealing has gone: stockbrokers are not all unapproachable people who will turn up their public school noses at sums below £20,000. They advertise on television and are happy to deal in just a couple of hundred pounds. Brokers are no longer the only way of buying though. Even banks, which used to deal through brokers for their customers, and then add their own fee to the brokers', are now smartening up their service, offering clients the technology usually available only to professionals. There are share-dealing companies operating by telephone or through shops too, but their service has not always been ideal and the government has been forced to close down many, with investors sometimes left looking for money from a liquidator and facing a loss.

Buying and selling shares has never been so easy – but it does put more onus on the investor to check first what he is buying and through whom. Just as in the supermarket, convenience has been provided at the expense of advice, and investors should certainly check both share prices and dealing costs at different sources before committing their cash.

They should not let this ease of dealing run away with their funds. Just as this century has seen most people becoming home owners, we are now seeing a move to share ownership – and with the same sort of Government incentives such as cutting the stamp duty. But just as home ownership is not the answer to everyone's problems, neither is share ownership. There are plenty of other uses for money – including spending it – and an over-commitment to shares can be positively dangerous. While aiming to help readers understand and use the stock market, this book does not forget the alternatives, whether it is in a fixed interest investment which protects capital, or a unit trust which allows the benefits of share ownership without most of the decision making. But this book is not only invaluable to first-time investors. As brokers' commissions adjust to the Big Bang, their free advice service is becoming a thing of the past. Consequently, this book provides all the relevant knowledge needed in order to trade successfully.

The City pages of *The Daily Telegraph* give a constant source of news on what is happening to individual companies, how particular share prices have moved, and how the mechanics of investing itself are changing. The Money-Go-Round personal finance pages each Saturday and Wednesday look at share investment along with other ways of making and spending money wisely. It is the broadest and most comprehensive range of such articles to be found in any newspaper. While daily pages can provide share tips and weekly articles can spell out some of the changes taking place, it requires books such as this to collate the information and to explain in greater detail, points that can be found in an easily retrievable form, which can be followed step-by-step or read in individual relevant sections.

The aims of these books is not to make readers into experts in areas that affect them only infrequently, but to provide the advice and information of experts when they do require it. As such, this book is an essential part of that service.

Richard Northedge
The Daily Telegraph Deputy City Editor

1 THE WONDERFUL WORLD OF SHARES

The British Telecom boom

Monday, 3 December, 1984 was the day the stock market gained acceptance among the British public as a place to invest money; 2,300,000 investors watched in amazement as their partly paid British Telecom shares, for which they had put up 50p each, started trading on the Stock Exchange. By the end of the first day's trading, the shares were changing hands at 95p each, almost doubling every investor's money. No matter that each individual was limited to 800 shares. Almost by magic, £400 was transformed into £760. And it got better. Two months later, the investors who had resisted the temptation to take a profit on that first hectic day had trebled their money.

British Telecom was the great British public's first serious introduction to the world of stocks and shares. Even allowing for the foreign investors and the people who subscribed for shares on several different forms using different names (and there were plenty who tried that and got away with it in a small way, in spite of the threat of prosecution), over two million individuals took up the Government's Telecom privatisation offer. Almost twice as many as the number of people who go to the cinema every week. There is a Telecom shareholder for every eight car owners in the nation. It still left Britain some way behind the United States of America as a nation of investors – share ownership is twice as popular in proportion to the population there as here. But nevertheless, the average British investor was starting to look beyond the local building society for his or her investments, for the first time ever.

British Telecom is now history. To be honest, the shares have never matched the performance they showed in those first glorious two months, and since then, relative to the rest of the stock market, have been a bit of a disappointment. So it probably reflects great credit on the average Briton that one-third of the private investors in Telecom unloaded their holdings in the months following its issue. The link between the private individual and the stock market is continuing, and growing stronger. If only because other issues, just as large and almost as heavily promoted, have followed. British Gas, TSB, British Airways, all made a minimum profit of 40 per cent for investors, within a month. More issues, be they government sell-offs or private companies raising fresh capital, will follow.

Like British Telecom, the British Gas publicity campaign included many months of television advertising broadly aimed at making the public aware of the company and receptive to the share sale when it arrived. Like British Telecom, British Gas generated Parliamentary questions, column after column of newspaper articles, and circulars by stockbrokers whetting investors' appetites months before the actual date scheduled for the issue. With profits over £1 billion, sales of well over £7 billion, over £100 for every man, woman and child in the country, and almost 100,000 employees, British Gas would rate as an industrial colossus in any country.

Private investors are also here to stay because, arguably for the first time in over a century, the stockbrokers who oil the wheels of the share transaction industry actually want them, and very keenly. The Government, in addition to creating new companies to float on the stock market, has stopped the commission fixing monopoly that allowed stockbrokers to get fat on a protected payment structure that gave all the richest rewards to brokers handling big investment fund, or institutional, business.

Making money on the stock market is not all as easy as subscribing to shares in British Telecom. British Telecoms do not grow on trees. Indeed there are times when almost every share in the stock market trots depressingly down-

hill, sometimes for years at a time. Individual shares sometimes drop in value so fast it is difficult to believe your daily
newspaper has not made a printing error. Some go bust.
Sadly, for a variety of reasons not totally divorced from the
gullibility and greed that is all too real a part
of human nature, these are just the kind of shares the
newcomer to investing is likely to own.

Consider retailing, back at the turn of the decade. A
newly elected Government was promising to cut taxes and
increase spending power. What more natural place to
invest than in chains of shops? What better shop to choose
for a stock market investment than the chain that just
opened in your local street? Two chains of shops stood out
as interesting investments, Dixons, the photographic retailers, and Bambers, which sold women's and childrens'
clothing. Both were expanding rapidly – Dixons up from
180 to 206 stores in a year. Bambers growing even faster,
from 160 to 200 stores. Dixons was more profitable, with
pre-tax profits of £10.7 million against Bambers with £4.1
million. But you could easily (and many did) just take that
as an indication of the considerable extra room for growth
in profits there was in the Bambers' chain. Also, as a closer
look at the two companies would have told you, Bambers
was not that far behind Dixons in profit terms by the time
you stripped out the property and manufacturing profits in
the Dixons' figures, and the profits being made by a separate, problem hit chain of pharmaceutical wholesalers
caught in the grip of a horrific and bloody price war.

An investor picking shares in both would, at first, have
had a happier ride from Bambers than from Dixons, as
the share price charts on pages 138–140 show. Bambers'
stores had glamour, had fashion, had an annual report
plastered with colour photographs and a kind of inde-
finable but vaguely exciting way with razzamatazz. The
annual reports read in a way that seemed to promise great
things in the future – no shortage of confidence by the
board showing there. By contrast, Dixons' annual reports
of the time seemed a little more, well, restrained. As well
they might. The pharmaceutical problems were worrying
the company, and the controlling family's elder statesman,

Charlie Kalms, had just died. You would have had to have been a pretty miserable investor to have run your Dixons pocket calculator over the two balance sheets, and discover that Dixons was moving its goods off its shelves and on to its customers much more rapidly than Bambers, and to worry that if either made a mistake in its buying policy, leaving unwanted goods on the shelves, Bambers would be hurt most. And even to care that Bambers had higher borrowings, making it vulnerable if a credit squeeze and higher interest rates came about. Or would you?

As the months passed, and the Bambers' directors dumped shares equivalent to 18 per cent of the equity on to the stock market and into the hands of other investors, a discerning and regular shopper would have noticed a gradual change in the quality of goods in the Bambers stores. Bambers was moving into shoes, a new area, and seemed to be becoming even more fashion orientated. But that did not stop at least one major stockbroker recommending the sale of Dixons' shares, and the purchase of Bambers. By end-1980/early-1981, both companies were announcing a fall in profits.

By end-1981 Bambers was dancing forward with considerable flair, opening new stores, planning even more, adding extra ranges of accessories, menswear and even some household textiles. But as 1981 passed into 1982, it seemed somehow to have lost its way. Its stores never seemed as crowded as those of Dixons, even allowing for the fact that Dixons was choosing prime high street sites, and the Bambers' properties were somewhat off-centre. Dixons, meanwhile, had discovered the deregulation of telephone sales, citizens band radio and, especially, video recorders. It was also acting very determinedly on the pieces of the business that were not working well, such as the pharmaceutical side, largely sold by now, and film processing.

The difference in the stock turns of the two companies, and in the debt position, was becoming even more marked. Meanwhile an even larger and more prestigious firm of stockbrokers recommended Bambers' shares as one of the most attractive in the retail sector. October 1982 brought the first clear parting of the ways. Bambers' interim profits plunged from £1.5 million to a loss of £3.9 million. The company said its stores had been badly overstocked, and it had got caught out holding too many goods the public did not want to buy. By this time, the stock turnover rate was up to almost six months.

A company with a stronger balance sheet might have ridden this, especially as interest rates were tumbling. Indeed, one major investment publication, and a prominent daily newspaper, went out of their way to recommend the shares, quoting in particular the attractive asset backing per share – nearly four times higher than the share price. But Bambers was in desperate trouble. It could not raise more money to buy fresh stock, so its stores were stuck with goods on the shelves that customers did not want, and as time went by would be even less likely to want to buy. It was so strapped for cash it had to pass its dividend. It needed to raise money, but found it had been expanding its shop chain in sites other store companies did not want, and properties put up for sale were not fetching as much as they expected. The company was on skid row, but for almost a year after this the share price was kept up by punters buying the shares hoping for a recovery to former glories. And also by gamblers looking for the takeover bid rumoured almost weekly in the press to be on its way.

The directors made more share sales. A buyer appeared, and put in a firm of top accountants to run through the books before putting down his money. This is by no means an unusual event. But while the accountants' report was never made public, it was enough to scare off this and all other bidders, and Bambers went bust in the middle of 1983.

Dixons, on the other hand, had hopped from citizens band radios and videos to home computers, and then equally deftly to word processors, and, in time for Halley's Comet, telescopes. Stock was in and out again, the company never staying long enough in any one product area to get caught with bad stock figures, never risking borrowing so much money that one very human error could cause its bankers to panic.

Since then there has been some controversy over just why Bambers Stores failed, and, just for the record, the company of the man who was hoping to take it over went bust too. But, that aside, what lessons are there to be learnt here?

First, do not always go for shares that seem glamorous. In 1979 and 1980, Bambers seemed a whole world more exciting than Dixons.

Second, if the directors of a company are selling shares, be cautious.

Third, everybody makes mistakes – you could say a board of directors that is not making mistakes somewhere is not trying hard enough. But the Dixons' board was cutting out its mistakes ruthlessly, and early. They survived, Bambers did not.

Fourth, high borrowings are dangerous. They make mistakes very much more difficult to recover from.

Fifth, take a cynical view of what the experts say. They may be right a lot of the time, but they have their problems too. Stockbrokers have to express new ideas, thus generating commission in order to live, and not all those ideas are going to work. Newspaper editors more often have a rising panic as the deadline nears and there is no decent story to fill the page. Under time pressure, it is all too easy for an inadequately researched story to slip through the safety net.

Sixth, use the specialist investment tools necessary for a particular sector. For retailing, stock turn is vitally important. For an advertising agency or a bank it is totally irrelevant. The simple arithmetical calculation of stock turn, explained in Chapter 7, would have been very useful in this case.

Seventh, keep a constant eye on your investments. An astute investor would have noticed the change in Bambers' stores, and their lack of business.

Eighth, apply a touch of realism to the hard figures in the balance sheet. If Bambers had been able to sell its properties at the price it thought it could, it would probably never have gone bust.

Ninth, shares are for buying and selling, not just holding.

A light-footed investor could have been in and out of Bambers' shares in 1980, making far more profit than he did from Dixons. Even after the news of the losses and the dividend cut had been made public, an investor who had failed to keep an eye on his stores but was objective about their prospects could still have salvaged up to 20p a share. The first loss is usually the cheapest – get out immediately if an investment has gone sour.

Tenth, every investor makes mistakes, as the many skilled and experienced people, both individuals and professional fund managers, caught in Bambers, can testify. If you cannot bear to admit you are wrong, or cannot afford the loss of a share going bust, do not invest. This is covered in more detail in later chapters. Even if you can, keep a sensibly structured spread of shares to minimise the impact of these losses.

So much for the moralising. Are these examples really untypical? No, they are not, these patterns are repeated by hundreds of shares every year. Polly Peck, on page 138, shot in three months from the equivalent of 30p to over 300p. Now you might think an annual rate of increase of forty fold was unsustainable – put a hundred pounds in and you would be a millionaire in just over two years. Lots of investors did not think so. That is why they were piling in faster than ever at the end of 1982, at the very top. The shares have almost halved since, while the stock market as a whole has doubled.

London & Liverpool Trust was even more spectacular. This took off from an almost identical point, 30p, and likewise broached the 300p mark with ease. London & Liverpool came down with a wallop, but unlike Polly Peck, London & Liverpool's fall did not stop. The company went bust. Like Bambers, investors here lost all their savings.

Everyone will have their own lessons to draw from these examples. But of the ten rules outlined earlier, the one about the realistic value of things in the balance sheet and the one about keeping an astute eye on the investment apply to London & Liverpool. Criticism in the trade press of its large screen television machines was surfacing even while the shares were at their peak, and the company's

21

method of accounting for its leasing contracts was there for all to see.

Disasters happen in privatisations as well. When the Government sold off Britoil at end-1983, the partly paid shares halved in three months. Not all State sell-offs are a licence to print money, you see. And no share, no matter how prestigious the promoter, be it Government, top rank merchant bank or whatever, can be guaranteed to hold its value. People sell shares for a reason, and it is always worth spending a little time trying to fathom out what that reason is. In the case of Britoil (and also other privatisations), it was because the Government needed the money, and the higher it set the price, the more cash it would get in. The seller sets the terms, and that alone ought to give pause for thought.

But when the seller is also promoting shares through the nation's 19 million television sets, and the number of stock market punters is starting to rival the number of people who go to football matches every Saturday, the time has come to do a little more than sit down and think. It is time to sit down and read, to grab a calculator and work out figures, to look around and to hunt out statistics, to work out ideas. Investment and the stock market have suddenly moved into everybody's living room, and it is to save people being caught out by the dangers of the investment world that this book has been written.

It has also been written to help people make money on the stock market as safely as possible, and to help people understand how the giant professional investment managers, who control 70 per cent of the money flowing in and out of the stock market every day, take their investment decisions. The amount of money the professional fund managers push through the stock market each day inevitably has a major effect on share prices. Whether you follow the same investment rules as the professionals or not, it is important to know the reason(s) why these managers take a decision to buy or sell a share.

Should you be buying shares?

No-one *has* to buy shares. Even the richest of people can, and sometimes do, go through their entire lives without gaining so much as a nodding acquaintance with a share certificate. Particularly in the 1980s, when money placed on fixed interest deposit with a bank or building society can pull in 5 per cent a year more than the inflation rate even after deduction of standard rate tax, buying shares is a form of financial luxury rather than a financial necessity. Buying shares can give you the chance of getting rich very quickly – if things go well – but it also gives you the chance to lose very quickly too. Avoiding so-called speculative shares will not necessarily save you from a big loss. Rolls Royce was a blue chip share, and it still failed (in 1971). Guest Keen & Nettlefold is one of the largest employers in the country, but between 1980 and 1982 its shares collapsed from 288p to 105p. After dealing costs, you would have lost two-thirds of your money, and if you had held on to them you still would not have got it all back. In June 1985, in the middle of a raging bull market, Racal shares lost a third of their value in just two weeks. My advice to all investors is to ask themselves, 'What would happen to me if my investment was wiped out completely?'

Let us examine the various points, one by one, that could influence a decision.

1 Can you mentally take the blow of having lost a large part of your savings?
This is not a financial question at all; it is a question of the make-up of your personality, and primarily a question of your own ego. If you make a mistake investing, it is your mistake – you made the decision, no matter who advised you. As that share you bought goes tumbling downward, even the most cool-headed and well-balanced individual feels that he or she has been rather silly.

Investing in shares is not a private matter, of course. Most people tell friends when they have bought a share. Suddenly your failure becomes known to the world at large, and all the people you have told are thinking (sometimes saying) smugly that any fool could have seen the collapse in that share price coming.

Some people cannot take that kind of failure without either going through mental agonies or exploding in some way. If you are still nursing wounded pride weeks after picking up a parking ticket, or are convinced that every shop assistant is intent on overcharging you, stick to a building society, or if you must, put a very small part of your savings in a unit trust.

2 *What is your future earning power?*

Conventional thinking tends to attack stock market investment from the point of view of whether you are rich enough to afford it. While a valid viewpoint, this does not actually go far enough. The younger a person is, the more risks he or she can take on investments, as the earning power of all those future years of work should make it easy to earn back any losses made on the stock market.

An 18-year-old, investing the savings from his or her first six months' salary, can plunge the whole lot into the most risky ordinary share on the market because he or she has another 40 years of working life left to make good the losses. A pensioner, on the other hand, just retired and with a large lump sum pension benefit to play with, has to be a great deal more careful, for all the extra money he or she has available. Once the pensioner loses that lump sum, there will be no extra money coming in to replace it. People coming up to retirement in fact, frequently look forward to the spare time they will have available to 'play the market'. It may be fun, but it is not necessarily financially prudent. If you are retiring (or are retired) a useful book to read is *Planning for Retirement* by Tony Levene, published by Telegraph Publications.

The same example applies to members of a pop group who no longer have records in the Top Ten, to people with redundancy payments, winners on the football pools or those who have just sold private businesses that they have built up after years of hard work. If you will not be able to replace the money you are investing, then be careful with your investment.

3 *What are your outgoings?*

This very much influences what we may call the 'cushion factor', money that needs to be set aside to meet potential problems that could occur while money is tied up in the stock market. A married person with a family to support needs a far larger safety cushion than a person who is single. Redundancy or serious illness eats into savings at a rapid rate even for the person with no dependents. Add a spouse and a couple of children (plus two cars, and private education perhaps?) and savings can be run through at an alarming speed. If your particular savings are tied up in a share worth half what you paid for it, and you are then made redundant, or are stricken with a stroke or a heart attack, you could be in financial trouble. The higher your overheads, the more cautious you need to be about investing in shares.

4 *Do you have a mortgage?*

Owning your own house with a £30,000 mortgage (the limit for tax relief under the Government's Mortgage Interest Relief At Source scheme, MIRAS) is the best investment you are ever likely to make. Even a mortgage above that can make sense as capital gains on the sale of an owner-occupied house are totally tax-free, whereas capital gains on shares are taxed above an annual trigger point in the £6,500 region. If you are living in rented property, you ought to be asking yourself seriously whether you are doing the right thing in contemplating stock market investment. Buy your own house and take the geared-up capital gain made by investing a building society's money in your own bricks and mortar instead.

5 *What kind of pension will you get when you retire?*

If you are within 15 years of retirement and your future pension is going to come out at any less than two-thirds of your final salary, instead of investing, top-up your pension payments. Your pension payments attract tax relief, your investments in the stock market will not. It may be less fun, but as a standard rate taxpayer with a pension you will be investing £140 for every £100 you would otherwise be putting into the stock market. How confident are you that the shares you choose will move 40 per cent faster than the market as a whole? On top rate tax, you can put £250 into a pension scheme for every £100 invested in the stock market, again as pension payments, up to certain limits, get tax relief against income, while stock market investments do not. There are some exceptions to this – Business Expansion Schemes (BES) or the Over-The-Counter Market (OTC) (most of them are losers and to be avoided no matter how tempting the sales patter might seem) and some company share incentive schemes. Also the Personal Equity Plan put forward in the 1986 Budget offers tax-free investment through authorised funds up to certain relatively low limits. Generally speaking, you cannot beat the rules of arithmetic laid down by the tax man. If in doubt, see your company pension's officer and ask about Additional Voluntary Contribution (AVC) top-ups, particularly the ones invested in building societies. If you are self-employed, see your accountant and do not fall for the slick patter of the nearest life assurance salesman.

How much money do you need?

Ask a stockbroker, or any financial adviser, how much money is needed before investing in the stock market and the answer you get may be swayed to some extent by the position of the person or firm you have chosen. Ask a big London stockbroking firm that is into the institutional investment circuit, and you may well be told 'over £100,000', a figure that happens to tie in neatly with the partnership's high cost base. A unit trust salesman may well say £1,000 or £2,000, as long as it is invested in his units, but choose a very much higher figure if you suggest investing in shares direct, by-passing his product. A bank manager may be subconsciously influenced by the desire to keep a financially valuable customer rather than risk having one of his better-off clients lose a large sum of money taking, what is in his view, an unnecessary speculation. Every one of these views has a certain amount of validity, but should not necessarily be accepted without further thought.

We have already examined the questions of whether you should be investing in the stock market at all, and if so, how much of your savings should be put into the stock market. The question of how much money should be put into the stock market is closely related to these two points. There are only two other areas that need examining; firstly, what is economic from the point of view of dealing costs and secondly, the need to keep a suitable buffer of savings in case your equity portfolio should be completely wiped out.

Let us examine the first point, dealing costs. These fall into four categories.

1 Commission to the stockbroker can sometimes be slightly inflated by the presence of an intermediary, if you are dealing through one. This will be in the region of 1.65 per cent. Some broking firms have a minimum commission level in order to discourage small orders. A minimum commission level of £20 will effectively penalise orders of under £1,500 each. The penalty cost is relatively small. A £500 share purchase will have to work just 3 per cent harder to make up the extra cost. The minimum is there more as an indication of the level at which the stock-broker will view your business as uneconomic. If you are likely to be dealing below the economic level, it would be better for both you and the broker to take your business elsewhere, for example, to a firm that has no set mini-mum. Stockbroking firms based outside London are usually happy taking smaller orders. The office costs and staff costs of operating in a provincial city are so much lower than those of operating in the City of London that they totally change the economics of stockbroking.

2 Stamp duty, which is a Government tax on dealing, runs at 0.5 per cent. As it is a percentage tax rather than a flat rate one, it has no influence whatsoever upon the size at which it is economic to deal.

3 Transfer stamp is another Government tax, but this time a flat rate one. It is so low though, usually just a matter of pence, that it can be disregarded.

4 The turn, the difference between the buying and the

selling price made by the marketmaker, is the same for a small bargain as for a moderate sized one. Ironically, the larger the bargain gets, the greater the risk of having to pay a larger than usual turn. This penalises the larger investor, such as the pension fund or the very rich individual, and the small investor gains a relative advantage from this. The average 'turn' has become smaller since 'Big Bang' because there are more marketmakers competing for business.

So, we have one dealing cost that imposes a slight penalty upon the small investor, one dealing cost that penalises the large investor and relatively speaking helps the small one, and a further two that are neutral. Dealing costs, contrary to investment folklore, are not that much of an influence on how much money should be put in the stock market.

The second area of influence, the need to keep a financial buffer, is very much linked to the other matters previously discussed in this chapter. A man with a large mortgage, a houseful of very young children and a wife who is not working, certainly ought to keep at least three months' net salary in a building society as a safety net in case of redundancy or serious illness. Someone aged in his or her fifties, with a mortgage shrunk by the passage of time, a frugal life style and no dependents, will probably be less concerned with the absolute size of the buffer than keeping the total percentage involvement in equities down to 50 per cent in order to limit the risk factor.

A single person, aged 20, with minimal outgoings and the prospect of a series of large salary rises in the future, need keep very little money in the way of a buffer. If his or her total savings amount to just £2,000, it would be possible to make a case for keeping £500 as a buffer (in case the car breaks down) and investing the remaining £1,500 in two different shares, £750 in each. A high risk strategy to be sure, but a strategy tailored to suit someone who can afford to take a high risk – as long, that is, as our 20-year-old is prepared to accept that £1,500 disappearing completely if the wrong shares turn out to have been chosen.

2 THERE ARE SAFER WAYS OF INVESTING

People often charge headlong into buying shares without fully considering other potential investment vehicles that may be more suited to them. Other forms of investment can be particularly worthwhile for the investor who is unhappy at the thought of losing all, or part of, his or her savings – as can happen in the stock market. The investor may have an unusual tax position, either in the very top tax bracket, paying no tax whatsoever or having non-resident status, in which case he or she may not be liable to pay British tax.

In this chapter we consider the different investment vehicles available. These are some of the factors that need to be considered when deciding which one to choose.

1 The likely yield relative to interest rates generally. There is no point in listing here the investments in a league table by level of interest rate as the rates change so rapidly that even a magazine, let alone a book, has trouble in keeping them up-to-date.

2 Your tax position. Some of the investments mentioned here pay interest before deduction of tax. So if you are low taxpayer, or do not pay tax at all, these investments will have advantages. Other investments have tax deducted from the interest before it is paid to you and obviously this is not to your benefit if you do not pay tax. Some investments pay 'interest' in the form of capital gains; if you are a high taxpayer then this is to your advantage because capital gains tax (CGT) is considerably lower than the top bands of income tax.

3 How much of the 'get rich quick' concept can be eliminated? And on the other side of the coin, how safe are the investments? The two usually (but not always) go

together. The great advantage of many of these investments is that you can be almost certain of getting back
most or all of your investments when you want. At the
same time you rule out the possibility of great capital
gains.
4 Dealing costs. The costs of getting into an investment,
and, just as important, getting out of it again, can dramatically change the arithmetic of investment. Shares, of
course, are among the worst of all investments from this
point of view. Other investments can be a great deal
cheaper in terms of dealing costs.

The mechanics of buying and selling also come into play
here. How do you buy into your investment, and how do
you sell out of it again?

National Savings

Each year, the Government is committed to raising large
sums of money by attracting funds into the National
Savings movement. To get money in, it has to offer attractive investment opportunities. Indeed, they can have such
great tax advantages that some of them are difficult to
ignore.Basically they come in five different packages.

National Savings Certificates

Current maximum investment is £5,000. There is no
dividend payment, all the gain comes as a capital sum at the
end of the period. There is no income tax or CGT to pay on
this investment.

Do be aware of the danger of pulling out of the scheme
early as you will sacrifice part of the growth you would
otherwise have had. Savings Certificates make a bad buy
unless you know that you can leave the money untouched
for the full five years. Sell during the first year and all you
get back is the purchase price, with no interest whatsoever;
this holds true for most series of National Savings Certificate issued. On the other hand, if you pull money out
early you know you will get all your money back, with a
little more beside from the second year onwards, which
cannot be said of some other investments.

It is not usually worth leaving money in Savings Certificates after the end of their official life. The value of the savings continues to accumulate, but usually not at the same rate as for new units available.

National Savings Certificates are particularly suitable for higher taxpayers, but are generally poor value for non-taxpayers because of the tax position.

Indexed Income Bonds

Again, the emphasis is upon holding these for at least a year. Repayment in the first year gives interest at half the normal rate. However, hold them for over a year and there is a guaranteed 8 per cent interest for the first twelve months, with an interest payment that matches the inflation rate thereafter. This is the gross interest figure – if you are not a taxpayer, you are not penalised. If you are a taxpayer, you will have to declare this on your tax form and pay tax on the interest.

The bonds have a life of ten years, and the maximum holding is £50,000. Three months' notice of withdrawal of money has to be given.

Obviously, these bonds are thoroughly bad value while the inflation rate is 4 per cent and interest rates on other securities are over 10 per cent gross. There will come a time, however, when inflation rises again, and to have a proportion of savings in an index-linked area of investment will make very sound investment sense. Do not write off these bonds totally – just leave them for another time.

Like conventional National Savings Certificates, these bonds are bought and cashed in at Post Offices. There are no dealing costs.

National Savings Income Bonds

These pay interest gross, and so are particularly suitable for people who do not pay tax, such as pensioners or children. Interest is paid on a monthly basis, which will attract pensioners in particular.

The minimum investment is £2,000, and above that the bonds have to be purchased in £1,000 lots. There is an interest penalty for the first twelve months, so this is only suitable for sums of money that can be locked away. Also, there is a three month time gap between giving notice of withdrawal and getting your money back.

The yield is 12 per cent and is paid gross. It is taxable however; you will have to declare it on your tax form and the net equivalent at the standard rate of tax is 8.5 per cent. There are no dealing costs.

For any investor with spare money, rather than petty cash, this obviously beats the National Savings Ordinary Account by a wide margin. Its main competition is not from the National Savings movement, but from building societies.

National Savings Investment Account

This scheme is quite similar to Income Bonds. The main differences are that the annual interest is added to the investment, rather than being paid out as a dividend or interest cheque, and that the minimum holding is only £5. The interest rate, at 11.5 per cent, is slightly lower. Full interest is paid in the first year, but if repayment is needed in that first year the interest rate is halved. Again, when you wish to be repaid, three months' notice has to be given.

Like the other National Savings' schemes, Income Bonds and Investment Accounts can be bought and sold at the Post Office. There are no dealing costs.

Premium Bonds

The minimum purchase is £5 and there is a maximum holding of £10,000 a person. The bonds do not enter the draw for prizes until they have been held for three months. There is no income tax or CGT to pay on the prizes.

The maximum prize is £250,000. In awarding prizes, the Government works on an 'average yield' which, for holders of large numbers of bonds works very much like the yield on any other security only, of course, you gamble on just how much 'interest' you get, if, any. The average yield is 7.75 per cent.

Bank deposit accounts

These accounts have tax deducted from interest before it reaches the investor, so they are not suitable for non-taxpayers. Interest rates have historically tended to be rather lower than those available through building societies. But there are exceptions to this general rule. Investors with over £10,000 usually move off the standard scale on to a rather better rate than that advertised in bank branch offices. The Co-op Bank in particular has a very good scheme paying interest as high as that available in any building society.

The investor has to remember, however, that the security of the investment with a bank has dropped one, albeit small, notch. A bank is rather more likely to go bust than the Government. No major clearing bank has defaulted this century, but many smaller banks offering high rates of interest have gone (and still do go) out of business.

Building society accounts

The standard building society share account, like the standard deposit account, offers poor value. The better deals are the accounts and bonds offered by the building societies that have strings attached – for example, you cannot withdraw your money until a certain time has elapsed, there is a minimum investment, or one of a number of other relatively minor drawbacks. Income tax is deducted from interest payments, so again this is not a particularly suitable method of investment for non-taxpayers, unless the convenience of the account outweighs the financial penalty involved. Once again, there are no dealing costs.

Roll-up funds

These magnificent investment vehicles are a kind of short term money unit trust. Originally they were started as a tax dodge – the income was re-invested in the fund and, by a loophole in the tax law, could be taken out as a capital gain. That loophole has long since been plugged, but what remains is a way for the private investor to gain access to the high rates of interest available on the inter-bank market.

The largest of all the funds, operated by Rothschild in Guernsey, has no minimum investment, although £2,000 would be a sensible minimum. Other funds have minimum investments, usually of £2,500 or less. There are no purchase costs, but the cost of running the fund, plus a profit margin, are taken from the fund out of the interest being paid into it. In general, the larger the fund, the lower the charges.

Interest rates between the funds vary, but it does not always pay to take the one paying the highest rate of interest. The fund managers can get a higher rate of interest by taking longer term securities. The funds with the lowest yields tend to invest most of the cash by lending overnight to other banks. Those offering higher yields tend to have a larger porportion of the portfolio in one month and three month term loans – again to other banks.

The speed at which money can be withdrawn varies between the funds. The higher the interest rate, generally, the longer the investor has to wait for his or her money. It is never more than a month. A further factor to bear in mind when comparing interest rates is that some funds are more lax about where they place their investors' money than others. Banks *do* go bust, and a wise fund manager will steer clear of those banks with suspect balance sheets. His competitor may not, and might lend to commercial companies in order to bump up his or her yield.

Insurance policies

Insurance policies in this context are an amalgamation of two factors. The first is life insurance, which pays a lump sum to your dependants should you die while the policy is in force, but nothing if you stay alive. The second is savings, using the skill of the insurance company fund managers as a form of unit trust manager. Insurance policies originally came into force as an excellent form of tax saving. The income tax breaks for the investor, however, have long since been removed. What remains are certain tax advantages for the life insurance company and the fund manager: a good life office will use these to enhance the return on the investments passing a little extra benefit back to the investor.

There is now very little point in taking out a life insurance policy requiring an annual commitment to saving. The amount of money that has to be sacrificed by an investor who tries to withdraw money early (usually anything under four years) can be so exorbitant that it is just not worth the risk. Life insurance itself – term insurance to pay out a set sum on death, nothing if one stays alive – is a very worthwhile thing, especially if you have a family or financial commitments, but as it is very cheap to buy, this kind of policy is not normally mentioned by life insurance salesmen.

For the self-employed, or the fully employed person without a proper company pension scheme, a pension purchased from a life assurance company is a very good and worthwhile investment. Contributions bear effective tax relief at the top rate of tax paid. But again, there is little point in any investor locking himself into an annual contract. The charges (very well hidden) are exorbitant, and people whose circumstances change can then find themselves shackled to a bad deal. A move out of self-employment into full employment, a decision to leave the country, or a divorce so that annual payments cannot be kept up, can make a regular payment pension contract a liability. Far better to buy the pension in single premium amounts, as and when needed. The costs are relatively low, and there is no problem about a possibly unwanted annual commitment far into the future.

Gold

There are three standard sizes for gold bars that are traded on the bullion markets. These are 400 ounces, 100 ounces, and 1 kilo. Even with the gold price down to below $350 per ounce, an investment in one of these bars soaks up a considerable amount of money. A 1 kilo bar would cost in the region of £8,000. Smaller bars are traded in two archaic measurements used in the gold markets and the Far East, but nowhere else. These are the 'Tola', a little less than an ounce and the 'Taile', slightly more than an ounce. The most popular 1 ounce gold coins are the Canadian Maple Leaf, which trades at roughly 3 per cent premium to its gold content – about £230, and a new coin from the United States, the Eagle. Premiums can go up and down, so calculate the real worth of the gold, and check prices from several sources, before dealing. Krugerrands, the South African gold coin that started the gold coin boom, have traded recently at 1 per cent below their gold content value, so gold investment in other bullion-sized bars has an element of uncertainty that goes beyond the bullion price. Insurance and storage costs need to be taken into account as well as the loss of interest from taking money out of an interest earning bank account.

There is no commission on coin or gold bar purchases. If anyone tries to charge you commission, do not deal with them. The gold dealers make their money by the difference between the buying and selling price, and you should be aware of the size of this before you deal. You should also obtain prices from more than one source – sometimes by using this method it is possible to find a seller who is offering coins more cheaply than someone else is willing to buy them for, and in this case you can make an automatic and very lucrative turn.

Most gold coins, and gold bars, will be chargeable for CGT if a capital gain is made. Rather more important, sales in Britain bear VAT if the gold is brought into the country, and this about wipes them out as a useful investment. You can, of course, buy them when abroad, or in the Channel Islands, or even conduct your business by telephone from this country and have the gold stored abroad. But if you do, be careful to have it stored by a bank of the highest repute. There have been several sad cases where so-called 'investment banks', storing coins for customers, have had the proprietor disappear to Brazil with the coins at a later date.

Gold is not safe in other ways; in the last ten years, the

price of gold has oscillated between US$100 and US$850 an ounce. It is currently at US$400, with no guarantee that there is any floor at that level.

This brings us to the negative point about investing in gold. Not only is there no yield, but it costs money to keep. Keep it in your house, and it will not be covered by your standard household insurance policy. Insurance cover, in case of theft, will be a substantial extra. Keep it in the bank, and doubtless the bank may charge for storing it. Also, insurance cover will still be needed, even though it is kept on bank premises. This will cost money, although not as much for gold stored in a private home.

The average share yield, the income obtained from dividends at a certain share price, is 3.5 per cent. The cost of keeping gold will amount to between 1 per cent and 2 per cent of its value. Gold must therefore rise in value by approximately 5 per cent more than the average share to hold its own as a worthwhile investment. And that is before the problem created by VAT!

If gold still interests you, see Chapter 9 for how to analyse price trends.

Unit trusts

Unit trusts have a great advantage. They enable you to hold a spread of investments for a relatively small sum of money and to participate in the stock market without the risk that inevitably comes through holding a small number of stocks. For this reason alone, many stockbrokers recommend unit trusts for clients with under £50,000 of investment money and who need to maintain a relatively secure investment profile. They have another advantage as well. On a whole, the average unit trust outperforms the average share – granted not by much, just a percentage point or two, but enough to make a cautious person think twice about investing on his or her own account. Unit trust managers are not the only professional fund managers who regularly beat the stock market average. If the professional investors are regularly putting in above average performances, somebody has to be putting in a below average performance for there to be an average at all. That person, it stands to reason, is the private investor.

The cost of buying and selling unit trusts is, if anything, slightly less than the cost of buying and selling shares personally. There is an average 'front-end load' of about 6 per cent that is made up of the difference between the buying and selling price. The cost to the investor is made up with stamp duty at 0.5 per cent; average brokers' commissions of, say, 1 per cent on both the purchase and the sale; the jobbers' turn (the difference between the buying and selling price of the average share to the stockbroker) runs at between 2 per cent and 5 per cent. From this you can see that the cost of moving in and out of a share can match, very easily, that of moving in and out of a unit trust.

The wording 'about 6 per cent' is deliberately woolly. The Department of Trade regulations on the difference between unit trust bid and offer prices is particularly vague and allows funds to alter the rules from time to time. Also, fractions of a penny in unit prices can be rounded, so it is important to check the bid and offer price spreads with a pocket calculator to make sure the particular trust in which you are interested does not have an exceptionally wide spread.

Trusts also take out an annual fee for day-to-day management of the fund. For most trusts, this is 0.75 per cent, a level that allows the average unit trust to make a very handsome profit for its owners. Unit trust holders, you see, do not own the unit trust itself. Some unit trusts, however, are currently charging 1 per cent plus as an annual management fee. Avoid these unless there is a very good reason not to. Remember, there is still the occasional rare bird on a lower management fee. The unit trust management companies charging a low fee should, of course, be encouraged.

Fees apart, how do you choose a unit trust? Look for consistent and sound performance over the years. Magazines such as *Money Management* and *Planned Savings* print regular performance tables. Do not just look at the performance league table over the past twelve months. A fund that has topped the table over this period might have got there by manipulating its portfolio, it might have had a genuine

stroke of exceptional luck, or the manager in charge of it might have been struck by a momentary flash of untypical and totally unrepeatable genius. So a twelve month record is just not good enough. Look for a fund that has done well over three years and five years. That does not necessarily mean having been the top performing fund in those years, or even having been in the top ten. A good sound performance keeping it in the top quarter of shares 'in its class' is what you should look for. It shows tangible evidence of a reliable, trustworthy outlook on life that is likely to produce a repeated above average performance in future years.

'In its class' – what does that mean? There are different kinds of unit trusts. There is no point in comparing a fund that is 100 per cent in Japanese shares with one that is investing in UK high yield stocks. Before you even get that far, you should know whether it is exposure to a foreign currency and an overseas economy you want, or a good high yield from shares in your own country. The managers of these two funds are not even remotely in competition with each other for your money.

Having decided the particular kind of unit trust you want, and having weeded out those with exceptionally high charges that have not compensated their investors because of lack-lustre performance, take a look at the portfolios in the different unit trusts. These are easily obtainable by writing to the managers of the unit trusts concerned and asking for a copy of their latest report. Are they the kind of shares you would buy yourself? Remember, when examining the portfolio, you are looking at a historical record, sometimes six months previously. If you would have been happy moving into the kind of share that the fund manager was holding at that time, then this unit trust is a possibility for you.

If the portfolio is made up of spivvy, fly-by-night shares and your idea of a balanced portfolio is a mixture of Marks & Spencer, ICI and BP, steer clear.

There are other points to watch out for in fund choice. The area with perhaps the greatest points to watch is high yielding units.

How does a unit trust fund manager obtain a high yield

for a unit trust? The first way is to search diligently for genuinely forgotten shares yielding well above the market average but where prospects for the future are also good. The second is to load the portfolio with poor quality shares that happen to have a very good yield for the moment – such as shares in companies heading for serious financial trouble that will give a good yield in year one, but are likely either to cut their dividend or not to pay it in future years. An example of this is convertible loan stocks in companies that are in such serious financial trouble that the 'convertible' element of the share is of little use; there is little chance of the company turning in good enough results for that loan stock ever to be worth converting. Avoid a fund loaded with 'junk bond' shares such as tea, rubber and third-rate oil companies, or an abnormally high proportion of gilt-edged stocks and other fixed interest securities that offer a high initial yield but have no growth prospects. Look at the portfolio, and steer clear of any unit trust loaded with these shares.

The size of a fund is important too. If the fund is very large, it will have little chance of beating the market average by a significant amount, if only because the task of moving around many hundreds of millions of pounds greatly restricts both the choice of available shares and the chance of buying or selling them at precisely the moment the fund manager wants to. At the other end of the scale are the very small funds which can create big problems. There are a number of reasons as to why they are small; perhaps they have been largely forgotten by the fund management group to which they belong – the task of managing them being delegated to the office junior – or long ago they were stuffed with stocks where there is now little or no hope of finding a buyer, and as they are probably making a loss are likely to be wound up or merged with another fund shortly anyway. Then – and you are really on to a winner if you can spot one of these – there is the small fund that is about to be manipulated by a fund management group to become the 'star' in the performance listings: this fund can be heavily advertised to prove the management group's expertise and consequently attract money for the entire group.

This is really quite easy to do. A fund management company can have, say, a billion pounds under management, a large enough sum of money, generating enough commissions to have a few of the more powerful stock broking firms treating it as a very important client. It will also have many different funds, some performing better than others. Then it launches the 'Baby Whizz Kid' fund.

The 'Baby Whizz Kid' fund, with a total size of £10 million, is the tiddler of the group. At this size it will be losing money for its managers. When the stockbroking firms are looking for fund managers to underwrite a new issue, take part of a placing, or a slice of an indigestible slug of stock that is being placed privately with clients to avoid sales in the market depressing the share price, 'Billion Pound Fund Managers' will go on the allocation list. The group will be awarded underwriting commission, or allocated a slice of the placing, in proportion to its value to the stockbroking firm as a client.

If the placing or underwriting looks to be of poor value, the fund will turn it down. If it looks fair value, but possibly a risky one in the short term, the fund will put the placing into one of its large, mainstream funds. If the placing or underwriting looks a stone cold certainty, either because the broker (or merchant bank) has misjudged the pricing, or the stock market has moved favourably since the price was fixed, or the 'Billion Pound Fund Managers' are owed a favour on account of a past howler the broker has put them into, then the 'goodies' are put totally into the 'Baby Whizz Kid' fund. The stocks from several accumulated brokers form a disproportionately large part of its portfolio, and performance really motors. Six months or a year later, with a rise in unit price that leaves all competitors standing, 'Billion Pound Fund Managers' will advertise the 'Baby Whizz Kid' fund, an implicit message underlying the advertisement being that all its funds perform as well as that.

Do not fall for the advertisement. Only invest when the new fund is started, and sell at its peak because by this time the stocks have ceased to be channelled in its direction and are either being pushed into another portfolio or spread (as they should have been in the first place) around all the funds managed by the Billion Pound organisation. The time to buy 'Baby Whizz Kid' fund is when the fund management group decides upon their next target to massage; and do sell when the massaging comes to an end. If you can spot both these entry and exit signals then you obviously have such a good feel for markets that you should be investing directly in shares, not playing round in unit trusts.

Personal Equity Plans

In the history of investment, it is unlikely that so much fuss was ever made over such a mundane investment vehicle as the Personal Equity Plan (PEP). For despite all the ballyhoo about encouraging people to invest on the stock market for the first time, PEPs have advantages only for people who are so heavily invested on the stock market as to have exceeded the CGT threshold which currently stands at £6,500 a year.

PEPs are annual contracts under which you can buy shares in UK companies without liability to income tax on your dividends or CGT on your capital gains. The dividend yield on shares is in most cases very low – the average yield is a grossed up equivalent of 3.5 per cent, so for anyone on the standard tax rate of 27 per cent, the savings here are small. Only for the top rate taxpayers does the financial saving on dividends become significant. As for capital gains, any individual is allowed approximately £6,500 of CGT relief in any tax year. Only those who have already exceeded this tax threshold gain the capital gains advantages of a PEP.

The ceiling on PEP investment is £2,400 per person per year. Note that a husband and wife can have separate schemes, both up to the limit, and that separate schemes can be run for successive tax years, so that the £2,400 limit, which may initially seem low, in practice can allow a significant sum of money to be built up over the course of the years.

The money must be invested through a PEP scheme run by an approved PEP manager. You cannot write to the

Inland Revenue and have your existing portfolio approved as a PEP investment, although you may persuade a PEP qualified manager to take the shares under his or her wing on your behalf. Both fully listed and USM shares are permitted. There is a limit of £420 or 25 per cent of the amount invested, whichever is greater, on the amount permitted in investment trust shares or unit trusts. It is also possible to hold small amounts of cash in a PEP, and in this case the interest on the cash also counts as tax free. In the first year, up to £2,400 can be held in cash. After that, it is a maximum of 10 per cent of the *total* value of all the plans held.

Each PEP must be held for at least one full calendar year, January 1 to December 31, in order to qualify for the tax reliefs. This means the qualifying period could be as long as two years (if you buy at the beginning of January) or as little as 12 months and a day (if you buy at the end of December). You do not have to wind up your plan once it has qualified but can allow it to run, reaping the tax advantages, as long as you like.

The relatively small maximum size of each PEP means that most PEP managers insist on having discretion over the investment. They choose what shares go into it, not you. Although you may find a manager who allows you to suggest the shares, and maybe even transfer over part of your portfolio.

You would not expect the investment community to pass up a trick and let you have a PEP for nothing, would you? No, not even though the fund manager or broker concerned is making commissions on the purchase and sale of the underlying shares in the PEP. Most charges are in the range of £20 to £30 a year, and you should not consider any PEP managers that want you to pay more than this. There are some other points to watch, as well.

First, at what rate is the commission on the underlying share purchases being charged? The highest charge ought to be 1.5 per cent plus VAT. Is a discount given on the purchase price of units in unit trusts run by the PEP manager? A good PEP manager will knock down the average 6 per cent turn between buying and selling price of units by 3.5 per cent, as otherwise it will be double charging.

Is an extra charge made if you want to exercise voting rights? This is bad, but some PEP managers are managing to get away with it. And is there a charge on withdrawals, or transfers to another fund manager? The PEP manager will be getting commission on the underlying share sales when a PEP is unwound, although he will not necessarily get any if the PEP is merely transferred to a rival by you. Examine the small print to see when fees are charged and what they are.

Overall, PEPs are moderately useful things. However, they do not justify the media hype that accompanied their introduction.

Investment trusts

Investment trusts are very similar to unit trusts. Both consist of widely spread portfolios of shares and both give a choice of specialist funds that permit the end user to choose whether to go into Japan, the USA, natural resource stocks, high yield stocks, or a variety of other sectors.

Investment trusts even have some advantages over unit trusts. The costs of acquiring them are lower than the costs of buying unit trusts – or so the investment trust managers claim. That claim is something which should be taken with a pinch of salt because investment trusts are quoted companies listed on the Stock Exchange, and to buy them you have to go through a stockbroker, paying both buying and selling commission, stamp duty, and a turn (which can be exorbitant in the lesser known investment trusts) to the marketmaker. However, over the longer term, investment trusts tend to outperform unit trusts. The reason for this is that investment trusts always stay the same size, and the fund managers never have to worry about new money coming into the fund, or awkward customers who want to withdraw their money just as the stock market is dropping and there are no buyers for any shares within sight. On the other hand, getting in and out of an investment trust, with the dealing costs of using the standard stock market system, can upset that argument. An investment trust person will argue his cause against the merits of a unit trust until he or she is blue in the face – *or* vice versa. The investment trusts probably have a slight edge overall in terms of performance and dealing costs, but not enough to be worth making an undue point about.

There are two areas where investment trusts are different from unit trusts.

First, investment trusts are allowed a great deal more freedom in their choice of investments. They can have a far greater proportion of unquoted investments. They can invest a larger proportion of their funds in any one particular share. But this extra investment freedom has allowed some trusts to commit monumental mistakes in the past. It is more important to inspect an investment trust's portfolio than a unit trust's portfolio because the risk of finding problems is all the greater. Also, an investment trust can borrow money to invest in shares, giving an element of gearing that is illegal for a unit trust.

Second, the vast majority of investment trusts have no fixed expiry date. As investors get into investment trusts by buying and selling investment trust shares, the actual portfolio of the investment trust stays unchanged; this means an influx of buyers and a shortage of sellers can push up an investment trust share price so it is higher than the underlying worth of its net assets. Conversely, it also means that a surplus of sellers, and a shortage of buyers, can push the purchase price to lower than the net asset backing.

There is a vast army of specialist investment trust analysts at the leading stockbroking firms, and fund managers at investment houses, watching for opportunities like this and working a form of arbitrage (i.e. dealing on two or more markets, buying and selling, in the same securities therefore taking advantage of the price differential) whenever they spot what looks like an opportunity. So the ultimate excesses possible in theory with this system tend to get ironed out. Even so, the calculation of the 'discount' raises a serious problem for the private investor. Buy an investment trust share at 90p, when its underlying net worth is 100p. See the stock market rise 10 per cent, so the investment trust assets become worth 110p. But if the discount of share price to net asset backing rises from 10 per cent to 20 per cent, the shares will go down from 90p to 88p, and the private investor has lost money.

The supporters of investment trusts see red at this argument. They point out, quite rightly, that it is possible to buy investment trust shares on large discounts, and sell them on small ones, so that the investment trust share price *outperforms* the market. However, this is an area which is best left to the professionals. So far in the 1980s, the average discount for the industry as a whole has oscillated from over 30 per cent to under 20 per cent, and there have been times when some trusts have traded within a whisker of their underlying value. Indeed at one time, in the 1960s, some investment trusts traded at a premium to their asset backing, justified by the argument, which all the professionals accepted with a totally straight face at the time, that good high quality management was worth paying a premium to obtain!

If any private investor wants to hold investment trust shares, then fair enough. But it is important that he understands that the investment concerns something more than the rise or fall of the stock market, or, for that matter, the quality of the investment management going into the fund. It concerns the level of discount as well. In order to judge the discount, it is as well to use a stockbroker specialising in the field, who has the computer models and the full time experts to monitor what is good and bad value from the discount point of view.

There are some investment trust shares that both avoid the worst excesses of the discount/premium to asset argument, and also offer exceptional benefits to high income seekers and low taxpayers and, on the other hand, to people in high tax brackets. These are called Split Level Investment Trusts and have two classes of shares. They have a fixed wind-up date, so there is a fixed link between the asset backing and the share price, because the two must end up equal at the wind-up date, if not before. The first class of shares, the income shares, collects the income from all the dividends in which the trust invests. It misses out on the capital gains or losses, however, because the shares are repaid at their original capital value when the fund is eventually wound up. The second class, the capital shares, does not receive any dividend income at all but it does get the capital gains accruing to the entire trust. So, if the stock market doubles, and the split level investment trust is invested in the 'average' share, then if there are as many capital shares as there are income shares, the value of the capital shares will treble.

The sums work like this. Capital and income shares each contribute £100, making £200 in total. The stock market doubles, so this goes up to £400, with £100 set aside to repay the income holders – £400 – £100 = £300 – thus producing three times the original stake.

The arithmetic gets rather more complicated after the trust has been in existence for a while. If the stock market as a whole has gone up, then the capital shares will rise and the so-called prior charge, the income shares that have to be repaid before the capital shares get any money, becomes relatively less and less important. The gearing element, the effect of taking the capital gains that would otherwise have gone to the income shareholders, then gets watered down, so the capital shares rise less violently in future. On the other hand, if the stock market falls, the income shareholders still have to be repaid as long as there is any money left in the fund. If the stock market falls so far that the cash put up by the capital shareholders is wiped out, then the capital shares still tend to retain a value, even though they are theoretically worthless. What happens if the stock market rises again? The capital shares might jump from a stock market value of a penny or two back to their original value very quickly indeed. Then they become a kind of gambling counter. And in some senses, all the more valuable for it, because a little gambling money coupled with a lot of very safely invested money can make a thoroughly sensible and, at the same time, very entertaining portfolio.

Meanwhile, what about the income shares of those split level investment trusts? If the economy is prospering and industrial companies are regularly increasing their dividends, a strange phenomenon happens to the income shares. Their yield is, to start with, rather higher than that of the average investment trust or unit trust, because they are collecting all the dividend payments that would otherwise belong to the capital shareholders. Dividend payments by industrial companies rise, and the yield the income shareholders gets rises too. After a few years, the holder of the income shares is getting a far higher yield than he could get on a gilt-edged stock, or by putting money into the building society. What is more, if the economy is still looking strong, there is the prospect of dividends continuing to rise in the future, something that does not happen with even the most carefully chosen gilt. The income shares become so attractive that investors start paying more than the issue price for them. But as the income shares are going to be paid back at their issue price on the wind-up day (remember that the capital gains are going to the capital shareholders), as that day approaches, the income shares will gradually lose value, until they reach the wind-up price. So the income shareholder gets given a big dividend with the one hand, but gets some of that taken away in the form of a reduction of capital value with the other.

This is, of course, a very useful phenomenon for an old age pensioner who is looking for a very high yield but not at all interested in what happens to the value of his capital at some date in the future when possibly he may be dead. It is a very interesting alternative to buying an annuity. It has many advantages for the non-taxpayer, because the income coming in is all tax-free.

Meanwhile, the high taxpayer will be finding magnificent attractions in the capital shares. Here, there is no income whatsoever to pay tax on, merely an increase in the capital value that, given even a moderately healthy stock market, will take place over the longer term, and hopefully, an eventual huge capital gain that will be taxed as such and not as income.

Split level investment trust shares are probably the most complicated instrument on the stock market. It is well worth the time and the trouble taken to understand them.

They are a rare example of two parts separately being worth more than the whole. What is more, because they are complicated and few people understand how they work, they tend to be available on the stock market more cheaply than they ought to be.

3   FIXED INTEREST INVESTMENTS

Gilt-edged securities

Gilt-edged stocks, like shares, need to be looked at in a special way if investment pitfalls are to be avoided. The gilt market has its own jargon, its own systems, and its own methods of analysis. The methods involved can get incredibly complex, a by-product of the tendency of this market to attract people with higher maths degrees and actuarial qualifications. This is a distillation of the way those professionals look at the market.

Gilt-edged securities are a kind of Government-sponsored loan stocks that are traded on the stock market. There is no stamp duty on gilt-edged share deals. Commission rates, if you buy them through a stockbroker, are low and should be 0.25 per cent or less on any deal worth £10,000 or more. The account system that allows delayed payment for equities does not apply here. Gilts are dealt under 'cash settlement', that is, you have to pay for them the day after you bought them. And there is no CGT, either of gains or relief of losses, on gilts.

It is possible to buy gilts through main post offices, via a scheme called the National Savings Stock Register. This is the most suitable way to buy gilts in parcels of less than £5,000 if only because stockbrokers' commissions on small gilt deals are high. Above £5,000, however, dealing costs fall proportionately, and you have the added convenience of knowing what you have bought, buying at a price you can more easily control, which makes buying through the stock market more desirable.

All the gilt-edged stocks with the exception of the index-linked stocks pay a fixed sum of interest, split into two amounts paid at six monthly intervals. (There is one undated gilt that pays dividends four times a year.) Most of them are paid after deduction of standard rate tax. As with most things there are exceptions – the one stock that has its dividends paid gross, is War Loan 3½ per cent undated.

War loan. Obviously this stock has advantages for those who are either non-taxpayers or who are non-resident. Conversely, because of these attractions, it usually offers a slightly smaller yield than its conventional counterparts. Taxpayers will often find slightly better value in the rest of the gilt list.

Gilts can be split into three basic varieties by the size of their original issue coupon. These are high-coupon stocks, low-coupon stocks, and stocks with an average coupon.

The high-coupon stocks are the ones that were issued when inflation and interest rates were at record levels, and the Government was paying far more than it is now to borrow money. Consequently, the notional interest rates on these stocks are far higher than anything available in the investment world at this moment in time.

These gilts, like almost all other gilts, are going to be repaid at £100 per unit. Obviously, though, the interest rate of 15.25 per cent on Treasury 15¼ per cent 1996 at the eventual repayment price would be too good a bargain to miss. And we are not the first people to have spotted this. Other investors have bought the stock up to a higher price, where the yield drops to nearer that on the average gilt. Not as low as the average, however, because for every £1 that the price rises above £100 represents £1 of capital loss that will have to be picked up when the gilt is eventually paid back by the Government. Treasury 15¼ per cent 1996, for example, may trade at £135, giving a yield of 11 per cent, at the same time as Treasury 9 per cent 1992–6 is trading at £100, offering a yield of 9.5 per cent. With nine years to run before both stocks are repaid, holders of the Treasury 15¼ per cent 1996 are losing about £1.40 a year in terms of the capital value of their investment, and that has to be offset against the higher yield.

So high-coupon gilts offer the fascinating phenomenon

of an above running average yield for the investor and a gradually reducing capital value. If you think this sounds familiar, you are right. Both split level investment trusts and annuities issued by life assurance companies work on a very similar basis. So for the retired person, looking for cast-iron security, as high a yield as possible, but who is not overworried about the worth of his portfolio in ten or twenty years' time, these represent an intriguing way of tapping the total pool of wealth to provide a higher income over the next few years.

The calculations on these high-coupon gilts are quite easy. The annual interest is the normal calculation you carry out for any kind of security:

$$\text{Official yield coupon} \times \frac{\text{Repayment price}}{\text{Current price}} = \text{Running yield}$$

Which in the case of Treasury 15¼ per cent 1996 at £135 will be:

$$\frac{15\frac{1}{4} \times 100}{135} = 11.3 \text{ per cent}$$

The more mathematically astute of you will have spotted that there is an advantage in having income now but losing the capital value any number of years hence. But that is a rather more complex matter.

The second class of gilt is the low-coupon group. Generally, these were issued in times when interest rates were very low, typically in the late 1940s and early 1950s, when successive Governments were struggling to hold interest rates down to 4 per cent and less. Obviously, the passage of time has eliminated most of the more extreme versions of these stocks, but there is a goodly smattering of them bearing coupons below current interest rates. The coupons on these stocks are, a face value, unattractive. So the prices have come down from the original issue price to the point where the yield has risen to the level where it nearly, but not quite, equals current interest rates. Nearly, but not quite; because the price has dropped, the gilt can be bought some way below the price at which it will be repaid. So the investor misses out on short-term income but gains in the long run when the gilt is paid off by the Government. The actual income received every year is called the 'running yield'.

The sums are similar as for high-coupon stocks. They can be calculated as follows.

$$\text{Running yield} = \text{Official yield coupon} \times \frac{\text{Repayment price}}{\text{Current price}}$$

Low-coupon gilts are particularly suited to high taxpayers because the annual interest payment, on which a high rate of tax is paid, is relatively low, and a good part of the reward for being in the stock comes in the form of a secure, reliable (in the long term if not necessarily in annual increases in the market price of the stock) capital gain. As we have already seen, on a gilt the capital gain is completely tax-free.

As a number of high taxpayers look for dodges like this, the price of low-coupon gilts tends to be a little higher than one would ordinarily expect on a straight redemption yield basis.

The third category, medium-coupon stocks, behave very much as you would expect a dated, tradable fixed interest security to behave. Redemption yields can be calculated in the same way as for high-coupon and low-coupon stocks, but the difference to the running yield will tend to be relatively small.

We have examined two of the three ways in which gilts should be considered. The third way relates to the redemption date. Obviously, a stock yielding 3.5 per cent but due to be repaid in two years' time is not going to be trading very much below its £100 redemption price. If you assume the average gilt yield at the time of considering the investment is 10 per cent, then any investor in this stock will be foregoing 6.5 per cent of yield for two years before being paid back, so logic suggests the stock should be trading 6.5×2, or £13 below its £100 repayment value, which is £87.

Let us take this one step further and look at a stock due to be repaid in 20 years' time. Here, on the same calculation, 6.5×20, the price at which the stock should trade clearly becomes a nonsense because $6.5 \times 20 = 130$, and if this formula were still valid holders would have to pay new 'investors' to take the stock away. In fact the very lowest this stock ought to fall to, even given a repayment date so far in the future that it will see us all into our coffins, would be where the running yield equalled the current market yield, which in this case would be:

$$\text{Correct price} = 100 \times \frac{3.5}{10} = 35$$

Although if yields were higher the price would fall further. In other words, at £35 this stock will yield 10 per cent, the same as the market average, but would make no allowance at all for the extra gains to come as the value of the stock gradually rises towards its £100 repayment level.

The length of time a gilt has to run to maturity obviously has a considerable bearing upon the price at which it should trade in the market. Gilts with only a short life ahead of them can be expected to remain relatively immune to the rises and falls in interest rates, and the glad tidings or woe on the economic front generally, because the cash originally put up by the first ever investor is due to be repaid in such a short time. The longer the stock is dated, however, the more vulnerable it is to rapid rises and falls in value. Indeed, with low-coupon long gilts, where the running yield is what determines the price rather than the redemption value, capital gains and losses can be made to rival those in the equity market.

So do not think gilts are necessarily 'safe'. Those unfortunate people who paid £103 for War Loan in 1951 and saw its value fall to £18 in 1973 would not think so. And conversely, do not scorn them as an investment for the faint-hearted and gutless. There have been times when holders of long-dated and undated gilts have made capital gains in excess of 40 per cent in a year! Make sure you choose a gilt to suit your own circumstances and the risk profile you have mapped out for yourself (see Chapter 10).

There are a few technical points that need to be gone into here, principally the explanation of the different types of gilts available.

Short-dated gilts. By the Stock Exchange's definition, these are gilts with under five years to run before they are repaid. Interestingly, the commission scales on these stocks have never been regulated by the Stock Exchange, even before the Big Bang.

Medium-dated gilts. These have between five and ten years of life ahead of them. They offer a happy medium between the near total capital security of the short-dated gilt and the wild short-term price swings seen in the longer dated issues. Stocks with a life in the five to ten year bracket are generally dealt on at lower commission levels than longer dated stocks.

Long-dated gilts. The commission charged by your broker will go up once you pass the ten year mark and the stocks become correspondingly more volatile. However, there is no shortage of choice. There are over twenty stocks in this bracket, and it is possible to buy gilts that will not be redeemed for another thirty years.

Undated gilts. These are the real gambling counters of the market. Three of these stocks, War Loan 3½ per cent, Conversion 3½ per cent and Treasury 3 per cent, actually bear dates 1951, 1961 and 1966 respectively followed by the small print let-out phrase 'or after'. *Or after* it has certainly been, and in all probability always will be.

The interesting point with the undated gilts is, of course, that you cannot do 'yield to redemption' calculations with them as you can with long and medium-dated gilts. The running yield is all you will ever get. These, from the capital point of view, are merely plays on the future trend in interest rates.

The yield curve

Comparing gilts of similar redemption dates is easy enough. But how do you compare gilts of slightly differing dates? And how do you view the condition of the gilt market as a whole? The answer is to plot a graph, with the redemption date of the stock on the 'x' axis, and the redemption yield on the 'y' axis. The result will give you a scatter graph where a line drawn through the average

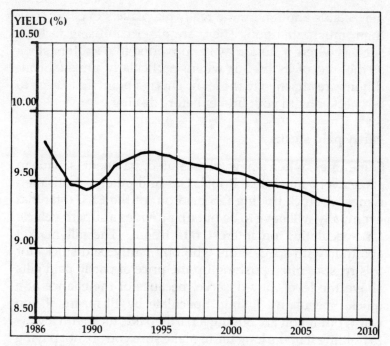

Figure 1   Government loan stocks – the choice of yields
The yield curve.

positions of the stocks looks similar to the one in Figure 1 above.

Your broker ought to be able to provide you with one of these, and any broker with any pretensions at all to a gilt dealing capability will have computers constantly drawing these graphs in his office.

The yields and dates tend to form a fairly cohesive pattern, and produce a line called the 'yield curve' (although sometimes it is almost a straight line, while at other times it has odd squiggles and bends in it). A good value stock will have a spot above the curve, a bad value one will have a spot below it.

Again, there are exceptions. Obviously, those stocks with tax breaks (such as low-coupon stocks and the ones with interest paid gross) usually tend to be below the yield curve. Issues where only a little stock was actually issued always tend to trade above the line because they are not

57

marketable enough for the really big players in gilts to pay them much attention. There are other confusing factors, such as where a stock may be converted into another stock at the end of its life, or where particularly unusual conditions are attached to the loan. This is a point that needs to be checked with your broker before dealing.

Partly paid stocks

Sometimes, when a new gilt is issued, payment is made in stages very much like British Gas and other privatisation issues. A stock trading £25 paid out of the £100 total that eventually will have to be put up provides a superb vehicle for speculating on interest rate trends. The gilt market abounds with speculators who buy partly paid stocks for this reason, often pushing up the price of partly paid gilts above the level they deserve, because of the chance of a quick, speculative killing. Speculate by all means if you want, but if you are buying a partly paid stock with a view to holding it in the long term, make sure you are not paying over the odds for the privilege.

Short-term trading

Move in and out (or out then in) of a gilt within 28 days, and you will usually pay commission only on the first transaction. Commission is such a tiny part of the total sum payable that you may feel this is not particularly important, but it helps.

Index-linked stocks

There is another variety of gilt, the index-linked stocks. These pay a basic yield, plus the inflation rate, to holders. There is surprisingly little choice in terms of basic coupon. You either have 2 per cent or 2.5 per cent in spite of the fact that there are 11 stocks in issue. Calculating the value of these is something gilt experts have several different answers for, depending on your assumption on the future value of inflation. But basically, if you think inflation is going to go back into double figures, these are stocks to have, and in that case you would not touch any of the conventional gilts with a barge pole. The fundamentals are so clear cut that you might feel the finer points of analysis would be a waste of time.

Other loan stocks

Any loan stock is only as good as the borrower's ability, or intention, to pay it back. So, while UK Government loan stocks are yielding 9 per cent to 10 per cent, it is possible to pick up a Mexican 16½ per cent loan at 'par', giving a 16.5 per cent yield. It is, come to that, possible to pick up 3 per cent Imperial Chinese loans yielding 25 per cent – only it is 40 years since a dividend was last paid and the value of the stocks lies in their pretty designs, which look very attractive framed and hung on a wall!

In between these extremes are a host of other bodies, such as county councils, loans from the now abolished metropolitan authorities, loans from dock and harbour boards, water boards and building societies. Now, a metro-politan authority may seem to you to be as good as the Government, but the fact remains it is not the Government, and as investors in the Mersey Dock and Harbour Board in the early 1970s will testify, sometimes these bodies do get into trouble, and the Government does not always come running to bail them out as quickly as one might imagine it would – or indeed, if it comes at all. Make allowance for that in the yield you are prepared to accept.

Do not forget that international bodies, no matter what their backing, are not the same as a cast-iron Government guarantee either. What price a loan from the International Tin Council, backed by the British and Malaysian Govern-ments, for instance? And what price an EEC Agricultural Loan if the Community members fall out badly over the growing grain mountain or wine lake?

Tax on accrued interest

The Inland Revenue assumes that part of the money you have paid to buy a gilt, taking 1/365th of the coupon between the date the last dividend was paid and the date you dealt it, is in the form of interest, and will tax you on this accordingly. The rule is:

Buy cum dividend – credit tax,
Buy ex dividend – debit tax,
Sell cum dividend – debit tax,
Sell ex dividend – credit tax.

These rules apply to British residents, and also non-residents if they are trading in the United Kingdom through a branch or agency.

DISSECTING A
CONTRACT NOTE

E.J. COLLINS & CO.

A.T.W. HARVEY
A.J. TYJAS

Associated Member
L.D. BROWN

STOCK & SHARE BROKERS

TELEPHONES: 01-588 7866
CABLES: COLLCOOP, LONDON, E.C.2

Friars House,
39/41 New Broad Street,
London EC2M INH
AND STOCK EXCHANGE

VAT REG No. 243 3882 57

BOUGHT by order of

ROBERT FLETCHER-SMITH

Subject to the Rules & Regulations of The Stock Exchange.

DATE & TAX POINT	FOR SETTLEMENT	STOCK OR SHARE	PRICE	CONSIDERATION (N)
08.08.86	08.09.86	5000 AMSTRAD CONSUMER ELECTRONICS PLC., ORDINARY 5P SHARES.	140	7000.00

Value Added Tax   N – Outside Scope   T – Taxable

		STAMP (N)		70.00
		C.S.I. LEVY (N)		.60
		COMMISSION (T)		115.50
		VAT		17.32
		TOTAL		7,203.42

Members of The Stock Exchange.

'XX207'

YOU ARE ADVISED TO RETAIN THIS
CONTRACT NOTE FOR CAPITAL GAINS
TAX AND VALUE ADDED TAX.

E. & O. E.

4 HOW TO GO ABOUT TRADING

You cannot just walk into the Stock Exchange waving your American Express card and buy shares from someone who has shares to sell. It is necessary to go through a stockbroker or some other specialist. In fact, somewhere along the line, a stockbroker is almost certain to be involved. You may find it preferable to deal through an accountant, a solicitor or your local bank manager, but an intermediary such as this will always use a stockbroker to buy or sell shares.

Trading through an intermediary can be very satisfactory. Tens of thousands of clients happily use this system, knowing that paperwork problems, capital gains tax (CGT) and dividend collection problems are being sorted out for them, often happy in the knowledge that their intermediary is using a very good firm of stockbrokers and obtaining excellent investment advice at the same time. But, particularly for the more active investor, there are advantages in dealing direct. There is less time taken before a transaction is completed. Because the instructions have gone through one fewer pair of hands, there is less danger of the dealing instructions getting muddled with the wrong shares being bought or sold.

Trading through an intermediary also carries another risk, that the intermediary will go bust, losing all your money. The Stock Exchange runs a compensation fund and, while not perfect, it gives the private investor a good chance of getting money back if the stockbroker defaults. With intermediaries, there are no such schemes. Obviously, using a major clearing bank is relatively safe. Using a Licensed Dealer in Securities or a member of an organisation such as FIMBRA can be fraught with risk. At the time of going to press, compensation schemes are operating, and there is a history of failure of this type of organisation.

How is it possible to know a good stockbroker from a bad one? Stockbrokers have been permitted to advertise by Stock Exchange regulations for years, but sadly, fewer than 20 per cent of the total have any kind of co-ordinated advertising campaign. Also, those broking firms that do advertise say little about themselves. The advertisements are by no means as revealing as those, say, for motor cars or insurance policies. Moreover, any stockbroking firm is only as good as the individual handling your account. A dense individual will make a dreadful hash of your investments no matter how good his back-up staff is, or the floor dealers who negotiate the prices, or the research department who provide the investment ideas. Choosing the right individual is by far the most important part of choosing a stockbroking firm.

Having said that, independent research has been published on the stockbroking industry and it is now possible to draw up several lists of various firms and their particular talents.

How to choose a broker

First of all, consider the market share – in other words, who are the largest in terms of UK business? If a broking firm is rated well up the size league, you can safely assume it has been doing a good job for other investors and increasing its market share, otherwise it would not be able to rise up this particular league. There is a disadvantage, however, in that the big firms tend to concentrate upon pension fund and insurance company business, where the big money is. The league table in terms of institutional brokerage commissions, which given the power of the institutions equates roughly to size, is as follows.

1 James Capel & Co.
2 Hoare Govett
3 Warburg Securities
4 Scrimgeour

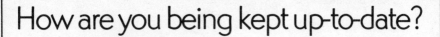

   5 Phillips & Drew
   6 Wood Mackenzie
   7 Kleinwort Grieveson
   8 Cazenove
   9 W. Greenwell
  10 Barclays de Zoete Wedd
  11 Alexanders, Laing & Cruickshank
  12 County Securities
  13 Messel & Co.
  14 Vickers da Costa (Scrimgeour)
  15 Chase Manhattan (Simon & Coates)
  16 Quilter Goodison & Co.
  17 Buckmaster & Moore
  18 Chase Manhattan (Laurie Milbank)
  19 Grenfell & Colgrave
  20 Capel-Cure Myers
Source: *City Research Associates*

Other independent studies have been published on the research capabilities of stockbrokers. These are voted on by the pension fund and insurance company clients rather than by private individuals, so again these do not provide the entire answer for the private investor. The two main surveys in the area have produced results as follows.

Extel survey
   1 James Capel & Co.
   2 Phillips & Drew
   3 Scrimgeour
   4 Hoare Govett
   5 Wood Mackenzie
   6 Alexanders, Laing & Cruickshank
   7 Barclays de Zoete Wedd
   8 W. Greenwell
   9 County Securities Ltd.
  10 Simon & Coates

Institutional Investor Magazine survey
   1 James Capel & Co.
   2 Scrimgeour

3 Hoare Govett
   Phillips & Drew
5 Wood Mackenzie
6 Barclays de Zoete Wedd
7 W. Greenwell
8 Alexanders, Laing & Cruickshank
   Warburg Securities
10 Chase Manhattan
11 County Securities Ltd.
   Kitcat & Aitken & Co.
13 Messel & Co.
   Scott Goff Laynot
15 Buckmaster & Moore
   Kleinwort Grieveson
   Savory Milne
18 Laurence Prust & Co.
   Panmure Gordon
20 Quilter Goodison & Co.

The finance directors of Britain's big companies are the subject of their own poll in which they rate the stockbroking researchers they come into contact with.

1 Scrimgeour
2 Barclays de Zoete Wedd
3 Phillips & Drew
4 James Capel & Co.
5 County Securities Ltd.
6 Alexanders, Laing & Cruickshank
7 Hoare Govett
8 Wood Mackenzie
9 Warburg Securities
10 W. Greenwell

Another way of rating stockbrokers is by the perform-ance of the unit trusts they manage. After all, if they cannot make money for the unit trusts run on behalf of their clients, how can they make money for anybody else? *The Times* and *Planned Savings Magazine* analysed the perform-ance of stockbroking unit trusts in 1985, compressing their tables to give an 'average' performance across all the funds for each broking house. This survey gives the following picture.

1 Henry Cooke & Lumsden
2 James Capel & Co.
3 County Securities Ltd.
4 Sheppards & Chase
5 Laurence Prust & Co.
6 Kleinwort Grieveson
7 Greene & Co.
8 Alexanders, Laing & Cruickshank
9 Scrimgeour
10 Buckmaster & Moore

Again, like all the analyses, these surveys contain serious flaws. Over the period when the survey was undertaken, US investments had performed badly, so any broker that had a US fund on its list of unit trusts had a serious handicap. A bit of luck can also make a great deal of difference to the performance of a very small unit trust. Even so, the Manchester firm, Henry Cooke & Lumsden, emerged a clear winner here.

For those interested in the USM, there is also a league table of stockbrokers in the USM new issue market. For any individual intent on following the new issue or USM market, a firm with a high place in this particular league table is going to have advantages. Since the USM was started in 1981, stockbroker involvement in flotations, either as sponsor to the issue or as official broker, have been as follows.

		Number of issues
1	Phillips & Drew	35
2	Capel Cure Myers	34
3	Simon & Coates	26
4	Alexanders, Laing & Cruickshank	24
5	Laurence Prust	21
6	Kleinwort Grieveson	19
7	Rowe & Pitman	18
8	Hoare Govett	16
	Barclays de Zoete Wedd	16
	L. Messel	16

11	Panmure Gordon	14
	County Securities Ltd.	14
13	Stock Beech & Co.	13
	Schaverien & Co.	13
15	Allied Provincial	11
16	Scrimgeour	10
	Cazenove	10
	Margetts & Addenbrooke	10
	Smith Keen Cutler	10

Some stockbroking firms have set up 'no frills' dealing services for the private investor, often with cut price commission and the ability to leave dealing instructions via Electronic Mail using a Prestel terminal. These include Barclays de Zoete Wedd and Hoare Govett.

Stockbrokers usually produce special bulletins for the private investor and mail them out to all clients on, at the very least, a monthly basis. These firms include:

Henry Cooke & Lumsden	(Manchester)
Pilling, Trippier & Co.	(Manchester)
Northcote & Co.	(London)
Wise, Speke & Co.	(Newcastle)
Henderson Crosthwaite & Co.	(London)

Other stockbroking firms worthy of mention, are noted below. These firms have developed special roles that are of use to the private investor.

Quilter Goodison & Co. has developed a chain of retail stockbroking units inside Debenhams stores, which make for easy face-to-face discussions for any investor living within easy reach of one.

Sheppards & Chase has a particularly large department specialising in dealing with accountants and other intermediaries.

Kleinwort Grieveson is probably the possessor of the largest private client department of any stockbroking firm in London.

A. J. Bekhor & Co. is a firm with an extraordinarily large number of 'associate partners' who act almost like self-employed salesmen, taking a share of the commission on every deal they handle. The firm therefore has a considerable number of private investors as clients.

There are also regional firms worthy of note.

Goodbody	(Dublin)
Illingworth & Henriques Ltd.	(Manchester)
Laws & Co.	(Bristol)
Murray & Co. Ltd.	(Birmingham)
Parson & Co.	(Glasgow)
Stancliffe, Todd & Hodgson	(Middlesbrough)

These six regional brokers have networks into James Capel institutional research and, as such, are able to provide a more wide ranging research capability than is usual for a regional broker.

There are over 200 British firms of stockbrokers who are members of the London Stock Exchange. This distinction is important, because while there are other stock exchanges in Britain – for example, in Birmingham, Manchester and Edinburgh – these do not deal in all the British-quoted shares. Any regional broking firm that is a member of, say, the Manchester Stock Exchange but not the London Stock Exchange will have to go through a London broker in order to buy shares in a company quoted in London but not in Manchester. The London broker will not do this for nothing, and this can often result in the investor paying a slightly higher commission. In these cases 'divisible commission' is likely to be paid. For this reason, many of the leading regional brokers have established offices in London and are members of the London Stock Exchange as well as their local one. Some, however, are not.

It is not always clear to the investor whether 'divisible commission' or 'best terms' are being paid. Quite frankly, the commission cost on a share deal is so small compared to the total, that many people feel it is not worth worrying about. But any provincial broker, accountant or bank manager will tell you if you ask. And for the curious, this is the kind of difference it makes on the 'old' commission scales that used to apply up to October 1986 and which currently forms the basis of commission calculations at most stockbroking firms.

Table 1

Slice of bargain	Commission	
	Best terms	Divisible
	%	%
Up to £7,000	1.65	1.65
£7,000–£15,000	0.55	1.25
£15,000–£25,000	0.55	0.90
£25,000–£50,000	0.55	0.75

A bargain worth £10,000 will bear commission at 1.65 per cent on the first £7,000, and, if on 'best terms', 0.55 per cent for the next three months.

It follows from this that splitting commission with a second intermediary does not matter as long as dealing sizes are under £7,000. Anyone who deals above that size, in the post Big Bang environment, will be regarded as a valuable customer and,ought to be able to negotiate a more favourable rate. But in any case, does it really matter? On a £20,000 deal, the commission on the two different methods works out as follows.

Table 2

	Best terms	Divisible
First £7,000	£115.50	£115.50
Next £8,000	£44.00	£100.00
Final £5,000	£27.50	£45.00
Total £20,000	£186.50	£260.50

A difference of £86 on a £20,000 deal can be wiped out by the difference between buying a share at 100p or buying the same share at 100½p. An astute dealer can make up this difference very easily and there is a limit to the amount any investor should worry about this. Even so, it is important to be aware that one is being charged for a service. Any investor dealing through an accountant or a solicitor ought to know that his intermediary is not going totally

71

unrewarded for his work, even if he is not charging the investor a penny for it.

A few more guidelines

Many large brokers who have commissions generated by pension fund business do not want small investors and therefore they have quite high starting points for a minimum portfolio with which they are prepared to become involved – £50,000 worth of equity investments is a commonly quoted figure. Those that quote a figure lower than this may give investors with smaller sums less attention than those with £1 million plus. Smaller broking firms and regional brokers will, by comparison, appear to lavish attention on the smaller portfolio.

For speedy dealing, it is often difficult to beat the very small London broking firm where the small private client is often given more attention than in a large firm.

Since Big Bang, stockbrokers have been able to adopt a dual role, also holding shares for their own account; it is as well to clarify whether the broking firm you choose is a market-maker or not, and if so in which stocks. Market-making ability might mean a conflict of interest – in other words the broker might put the need to dump some of the firm's excessive stock of shares ahead of the interests of his client. This conflict of interest can also apply to official brokerships – but to a lesser extent. Again, when choosing a broker, ask for a list of companies to which it is official broker. There can be benefits in being close to a reliable source of information on these companies, but there can be disadvantages too.

Ask your broker what research and other information he is prepared to send you, for example, Extel cards, annual reports and printed research notes on the shares the firm has recommended to you. Will it provide the occasional Extel card on companies in which you are interested, but in which the broker has no expertise? (Not even the largest firm of brokers knows what is happening outside the tiny proportion of shares in which it specialises in the market.) What research, if any, will it send you as a matter of course

to help you decide where next to invest? And is it prepared to lodge new issue applications for you?

Licensed Dealers in Securities also make markets in shares. These are financial organisations, approved by the Department of Trade, which offer to buy and sell shares both in Stock Exchange quoted companies and less reputable 'Over-The-Counter' (OTC) stocks. Ignore the OTC stocks. They have been consistently out-performed by the main stock market. Licensed dealer quotations in fully listed securities can be useful in the case of a new issue, as they frequently start trading a day or two ahead of the main stock market. They can, occasionally, offer a good deal on other stocks because they buy a bundle of shares at the beginning of a day's trading and quote a steady price throughout the day, whether the market is rising or falling, until all the shares have been sold. Usually, they do not charge extra commission but it is worthwhile seeking written verification. Bear in mind that those shares will probably have been bought from the official Stock Exchange, via a stockbroker who will have been paid commission, so it is very difficult for a licensed dealer to offer terms that are consistently better than a stockbroker. Also if the share price on the main Stock Exchange rises, the dealer's stock of securities will soon be exhausted by bargain hunters (or the dealer might decide to stop selling to the customer, and trade them back to the Stock Exchange at a profit). While if the price on the main Stock Exchange falls, the stock offered by the licensed dealer might be left looking rather expensive by comparison, unless the dealer follows suit by lowering his share price, absorbing the loss.

Most important of all, and as mentioned earlier, these organisations have an unfortunate habit of going bust, losing investors' money. The rule should be: *never, never*, deal with an organisation whose base is outside mainland Britain. The frauds that have been committed from organisations based overseas, including, regrettably, the Isle of Man, are too numerous to mention.

How to deal

Before accepting you as a client, a stockbroking firm is likely to ask for a banker's reference. Unknown to you, it will also conduct some elementary credit checks, such as making sure you have never defaulted on a Stock Exchange bargain in the past, or have been named by the police as being wanted for fraud. But once accepted as a client, what are the technicalities of dealing?

Once you and your stockbroker have decided on the share you would like to buy, ask him to check a price for you. If it is a small company, or you are investing a large sum of money, you should ask him to check out the size of the company stock as well because there may not be enough shares available to meet any order you may give.

Your broker will dial up the share on the Stock Exchange's closed circuit share price system (SEAQ). This displays the buying and selling prices, and the maximum sizes being quoted by each marketmaker. If you are dealing within the maximum size quoted, your broker will simply ring the marketmaker with the cheapest quote, confirming the price and the deal. If you intend to buy more than the normal market size, your broker may ring several other marketmakers and try bargaining with them.

Each marketmaker may quote different prices for different sizes and, at the end of his investigation on your behalf, the dealer may end up with a situation like this.

Marketmaker 1
58–63 in 5,000 shares.
56–65 in 10,000 shares.
Marketmaker 2
60–65 bid for 10,000, offered 2,500.
Marketmaker 3
55–60 in 2,500 shares.
Marketmaker 4
56–61 in 2,500 shares, offered 10,000, possibly more.

Unless you particularly ask for it, the information will not come back to you in this form. The dealer will pass it back as, '60 choice for 2,500, with 60–61 in 10,000'. The choice price means that as long as the client (you) wants only 2,500 shares, the price is the same for both a buyer and a seller, an unusual occurrence. Even more unusual is where the marketmakers are so out of touch with each other that it is possible to buy more cheaply than it is possible to sell, giving an automatic profit. This is called a 'backwardation'. Amazingly, before October 1986 it was technically against Stock Exchange rules for a broker to deal on one of these, even though it was in his client's best interests. Happily that has now changed.

You may decide 2,500 shares is not enough and want to buy 5,000. In which case you give your order to buy 5,000 shares at '61p, or better', a useful phrase to add because you never know whether the dealer might be able to knock his chosen market-maker down a bit.

Shortly afterwards the broker will confirm that the bargain (purchase) has taken place. The next day a 'Contract Note' will arrive. This informs you of the total cost of the transaction, number and name of the shares bought (and sold), and the date when settlement is due. Study the contract note carefully. If a mistake has been made, now is the time to correct it. There is no need to send any money at this point. The Stock Exchange works on a fortnightly 'Account' system. All the money owing by each client is totted up at the end of this fortnightly period. The money owed from share sales is deducted to give a net total. Sometime during the next fortnight a statement will arrive, repeating just how much you owe for the fortnightly Stock Exchange account just ended, and the date for settlement. The stockbroker will need his cheque in advance by the due settlement day – please allow adequate time for the post.

The mechanics of dealing in shares, however, are about the least important part of the whole business. The important thing is to make sure that most of the shares you buy go up, and that very few of them go down.

In any case, any attempt to master the intricacies of Stock Exchange regulations and the ritual of the market place is doomed to failure. Because of Big Bang, the rules are changing faster than you will be able to memorize them. Once again, Big Bang will have little or no impact on whether you make or lose money on the stock market. But it may have been causing agonies to your stockbroker. The following section will help you to understand the traumas he is going through.

'Big Bang' – its effect on investors

The Big Bang has nothing to do with analysing shares, but the changes to the stockbroking community that go under this name have made considerable alterations to the way ordinary investors are able to buy and sell shares.

The Stock Exchange is central to Britain's economy, and it is periodically subjected to outside investigations by Royal Commissions, Government departments and the like to check that it has effectively been doing its job for the country. It usually emerged with more praise than blame. The 1878 Royal Commission, for example, found that the body governing the Stock Exchange 'acted uprightly, honestly and with a desire to do justice'. The Commission also praised its 'rules for the enforcement of fair dealing and the repression of fraud, capable of affording relief and exercising restraint far more prompt and often more satisfactory than any within reach of the courts of law'. The Wilson Commission, a century later, also painted the Stock Exchange whiter than white.

In 1984, however, part way through another Government investigation, which had been dragging on for some time, it became clear that the Stock Exchange was coming out of the affair in a poor light. Fixed levels of brokers' commissions, so that investors were forced to pay the same costs for dealing no matter which broker they used, was, in some eyes, abuse by an over-rich, self-satisfied monopoly, and this was one of the bones of contention. Another concern was access to Stock Exchange membership: stockbroking firms could only be set up by private individuals who were already members and therefore, so to speak, 'in the club'. But there were other areas of criticism too. The end result was the Stock Exchange became aware that it was on the losing side and, about to have possibly quite undesirable changes forced upon it, looked for a way out.

At the same time there was further pressure on the Stock

Exchange establishment from another quarter. The London market, for centuries accustomed to being the world's stockbroker, was losing business to foreign competition; instead of London handling massive business transactions in North American railroad and industrial stocks, as happened between the wars, it was the American brokers who were increasing their business by trading in British shares. And not just for American investors – they were trading for British institutions as well! By 1984, over 10 per cent of the equity of companies, such as ICI and Glaxo, was in the hands of American Depository Receipts (ADR). (An 'ADR' is a package of shares which can be legally owned by United States nationals.) Indeed it went further, as it was thought that on some days over half the business in the shares of ICI and Glaxo was being transacted by American brokers.

It was painfully clear why British fund managers were trading overseas – it was cheaper. Not only were there lower dealing taxes, or stamp duty, but commissions were lower too. (The US investment community swept away minimum commissions in the mid-1970s.) Firms specialising in institutional business were able to charge very much lower commissions for big pension fund orders than they had before. After all, it does not cost any more to handle a £10 million transaction in a multi-national company share than it does a £10,000 one. This lower commission charge was brought about because big New York investment houses were acting as both broker and jobber. They were buying stock from one customer and selling it to another, making a turn in between, and on top of that they were charging commissions as well. Naturally they could afford to cut costs as long as they did not get their 'book' wrong and end up making a loss on their position. Commissions for private investors dealing in America were cut right back, but it is doubtful that the British investment community took much notice of that at the time: we were more concerned with how to stop the leakage of special, highly profitable, big fund business going to this new American competition.

The ground was ripe for a compromise. Whether the first

initiative came from the Government or from the Stock Exchange is hardly relevant, but Cecil Parkinson and Stock Exchange chairman, Sir Nicholas Goodison, met and some common ground was reached. There were elements on both sides that called it a sell-out, so the deal cannot have been too lop-sided. The upshot of it was the fixed scale of commissions was to be abolished, ownership of stock-broking firms was to be relaxed, on the principle that 'if you can't beat them, join them', and overseas stockbrokers were to be allowed direct access to the London market.

The deal was voted through, probably before the average British stockbroker had become fully aware of what had happened in America. In New York, commissions on institutional bargains had more than halved following the abolition of minimum commissions: for those broking firms taking a strong position in marketmaking, the cry was occasionally, 'commission, what commission?' Meanwhile the smaller stockbroking firms in London were looking with great interest at what had been happening to private client broking firms in New York. Some, by stripping themselves of the expensive research departments that stockbroking firms were traditionally expected to provide, and by eliminating the long, avuncular conversations with client liaison officers, were able to cut commissions for small private clients considerably – and advertise staggeringly low commission rates in the newspapers to bring in business. The commission rates may have seemed frighteningly low, but the private client brokers in London became aware that here was a method of doing business that they had never before tried. For example, in New York some private client brokers were advertising bargains at a *flat $30 per bargain*, no matter what the size, and at the same time getting their own back on the big brokers by coaxing away institutional business.

It soon became clear to the institutionally-orienatated brokers that if they were going to compete with New York effectively, they would have to make books in the shares they were trading as well as in broking. The middle man would have to be cut out, and 'marketmaking books' run on the massive sizes that the pension funds wanted. This new way of 'book' operations would contrast with the relatively small size of books operated by the few, privately owned, jobbing firms on the traditional UK stock market. The dividing line between marketmakers and brokers (broker dealing with marketmaker on the floor of the Exchange, carrying out clients' instructions to buy and sell in effectively a closed market) that the compromise hammered out with Parkinson had left sacrosanct, would have to go.

By this time, brokers, the Government and newspaper commentators alike had become so punch drunk with all the changes that this one was swept through without the serious discussion it probably merited. After all, had serious discussion taken place then they would have seen that the scandals at Lloyd's had come about because the boundary line between insurance broking and insurance underwriting had become blurred, and, by comparison, the separation of marketmaking and broking functions on the London market had kept share dealing mercifully scandal free.

It is worth pointing out at this juncture that the London stockbroking community has happily been handling more than one function at the same time for many years. Stockbrokers, who earn their living by generating commissions, have happily run discretionary funds for private clients, and unit trusts, which depended for their good performance on resisting the brokers' blandishments of the latest commission-generating 'stock of the day'. Brokers accepted fees from companies whose shares were quoted, to act as 'official broker', and either look after a company's interests on the stock market, or puff up its share price, depending which point of view you take. Stockbrokers were permitted to sit on the boards of public companies as directors (and still are), and promote those shares to their stockbroking clients. By the time Big Bang came on the horizon even the separation of marketmaking and broking functions was looking hazy. Some broking firms were competing against each other for placings in large lines of shares by quoting firm, competitive prices before they had a watertight buyer via the jobbing system, the old name for marketmaking, on the other side. They were finding buyers themselves, letting a jobber 'front' the business in the same way as happens at Lloyd's, by an arrangement called a 'put-through'. If buyers for the whole stock could not be found, then the difference was sometimes met by buying it personally as partners, with the partners' pension fund, or putting it into the portfolios of the discretionary fund clients.

It is also worth remembering that for three-quarters of its existence, the London Stock Exchange has existed with only the haziest of distinctions between marketmaking and broking, and also without a fixed commission scale. It was as late as 1908 when the separation between jobbing and broking was introduced. However, it took until 1912, after two years of heated debate followed by a vote carried by the narrowest of margins, before the free-for-all in commissions was done away with and a firmly policed minimum cost per bargain was introduced.

So, is mixed capacity such a revolution? And what does this really mean as far as the private investor is concerned? The first point is that from now on, thankfully, the smaller investor will be able to do business with broking firms that actually want his business, rather than firms that take him on sufferance because they were tied to a fixed commission scale and a narrow-minded business outlook that, between them, made business unprofitable. From October 1986, the rules that created these conditions have been abolished and, as brokers learn to use their new-found freedoms, private investors may be able to choose between low commissions and a no-frills service offering the minimum of research – possibly even a fixed price per bargain – and a somewhat higher commission from a firm that offers a good level of research, plus a personal contact who will stop long enough for a decent chat every time you, the client, have a problem. Institutions are dramatically trimming the number of stockbroking firms with which they do business. The result is that in many firms where private clients were the unprofitable poor relation to the pension fund trades, they are becoming the sole source of income.

Commissions being paid by the big institutions have been cut dramatically. In many cases institutions are trading direct with marketmakers, cutting out broking commissions completely. These conditions should encourage broking firms actively to seek out private clients to replace the profits lost as the institutional business becomes more and more cut-throat.

What difference has this made to the choice of shares available to investors? Before Big Bang there were fears that market ability in small companies would dry up. Mercifully, the reverse has been the case. So many new marketmakers have been established that there is more chance of making a market among small companies rather than less. For the time being at least, small investors can buy shares in small companies quite happily.

Another side-effect of Big Bang, which has not yet arrived, is on-screen dealing. The theory is that brokers will be able to look at prices quoted by a whole string of marketmakers on their VDU screens, choose the cheapest price and by pushing a button on the TV screen, execute a bargain.

In theory, this has happened already. Since Big Bang, marketmakers have supposedly had to stick to the prices quoted on SEAQ for the two largest groups of shares, Alphas and Betas. But it takes a telephone call to consummate the deal, and marketmakers have the right to plead a technical malfunction for a number of reasons. However, push-button dealing will change that. On-screen dealing should bring about narrower differences between buying and selling prices for the leading shares. Therefore close analysis of the top shares, and a decisive approach to buying and selling, should pay dividends.

The screen-based dealing system rapidly proved so efficient that the floor of the Stock Exchange became redundant, and even before its formal closure, little used.

All in all, Big Bang has brought a mixed bag making life more interesting. It is with this in mind that we examine, step-by-step, the routes to take in choosing the right shares to buy.

5 SO MANY MARKETS TO CHOOSE FROM

Britain supplies only 5 per cent of the capitalist world's Gross National Product (GNP). And in an international age, when many markets are competed for by companies on a world-wide scale and many British companies view their principal competitors as being foreign instead of from the UK, it is very necessary to look on investment from a global viewpoint and not a purely British one.

You may be tempted to buy shares in a chemical company, for instance. In Britain that amounts to ICI, with a market capitalisation of £9 billion, and then the next largest company that can truly be called chemical, as distinct from industrial gases or paint manufacturing, is Laporte, with a market capitalisation of only £700 million. But does ICI dominate the British chemical market? Not a bit of it. Its main competitors in the British market are products that are either imported (if currencies are moving in the right direction) or made at British factories owned by foreign companies. Companies such as Du Pont, and Monsanto, both USA companies, Bayer, Hoechst and BASF of West Germany, Montedison of Italy, Rhone Poulenc of France, and Mitsubishi of Japan. Every one of these companies is as large, give or take a billion or so, as ICI. It is a sobering thought that West Germany, a country with roughly the same population as Britain, can muster three chemical companies that bear comparison with ICI, on almost any criteria you care to name.

ICI gains some advantage, of course, in its home market. But then, is Britain really ICI's home market? The company has a massive manufacturing base in the US – it makes 20 per cent of its world output in factories there. It has factories, either wholly or partly owned, in over a dozen other countries around the world: with over 60 per cent of its output being sold in countries other than Britain. So clearly, following the state of the British chemical market is far from the complete answer to guessing what is going to happen to ICI's profits. And watching movements made by ICI's nearest British competitor, Laporte, in terms of price changes, new product releases, etc., and hoping to gain an insight into what is happening at ICI as a result, is clearly pointless when the real competition for ICI is BASF,

Table 3   World chemical companies

Position	Company	Country	Sales US$bn	Profits US$bn	Number of employees
1	Du Pont	USA	15.9	1.1	124,893
2	Bayer	W. Germany	13.4	0.4	174,755
3	BASF	W. Germany	12.8	0.3	115,816
4	Hoechst	W. Germany	12.5	0.4	177,940
5	ICI	Britain	11.5	0.7	115,600
6	Dow Chemical	USA	11.4	0.6	49,800
7	Union Carbide	USA	9.5	0.3	98,366
8	Shell*†	European	6.9	0.4	27,000
9	Exxon*†	USA	6.9	0.4	18,000
10	Ciba-Geigy	Switzerland	6.7	0.5	81,423
11	Monsanto	USA	6.7	0.4	50,754
12	Montedison	Italy	6.4	–	72,215
13	DSM	Holland	6.3	0.1	27,190
14	Rhone Poulenc*	France	5.3	0.2	80,120
15	Elf Aquitaine	France	4.8	0.1	38,601

Notes
*Non-quoted companies.
†Shares in their oil parent company can be purchased.
The league table of world chemical companies, compiled annually by the newsletter *Chemical Insight*, shows what extraordinary choice there is for the investor wanting to buy shares in a large chemical company. Taking 1984 figures, there were 14 companies with sales of over US$5 billion, and only one of them was British. You can buy shares in all but three of them, and with two of these† you can buy shares in their oil company parents.

Bayer, Hoechst, Du Pont, Montedison, Rhone Poulenc, Mitsubishi, not to mention the giant chemical exporters of Eastern Europe and the Middle East.

The same applies to any number of other industries you care to name. Britain's largest pharmaceutical company, Glaxo, barely creeps into the world pharmaceutical 'top ten' companies when measured in terms of turnover or profit. Although when compared to stock market capitalisation, strangely, it is the largest pharmaceutical company in the world. Wellcome Foundation, for all the excitement generated by its stock market floatation in 1985, barely makes the top twenty. In analysing Glaxo, should you be looking at Wellcome Foundation as a comparison? Yes, partly, but Gaxo and Wellcome hardly compete against each other in a single pharmaceutical product area worth speaking of. Far more important are the US giants Smithkline, whose Tagamet anti-ulcer drug is a major competitor to Glaxo's Zantac, or Eli Lilly, whose bulk antibiotic interests are a major influence on a marketplace where Glaxo also heavily competes.

Many pharmaceutical companies, for example, the three Swiss giants Ciba Geigy, Hoffmann La Roche and Sandoz (again each of them roughly Glaxo's size, or bigger) sell over 90 per cent of their products in countries that are to them 'overseas'. Also, to oil companies, countries of origin are almost irrelevant.

Even industries that appear entirely domestic are usually subjected to overseas influence. Take another example, employment agencies. A boom in the temporary secretary market might find you poring over the annual report of Blue Arrow, which with the Brook Street Bureau and Reliance chains, is Britain's largest quoted employment agency company. Who does Blue Arrow regard as its main competitors in the British market? Why, Kelly Girl and Manpower, both of which dwarf Blue Arrow in size internationally, and both of which are quoted on American stock exchanges. Before buying Blue Arrow shares, you would have to make sure it was not losing ground in the British market to these two, and check to make sure the shares of Kelly Girl and Manpower did not offer better value.

There are the movements of overseas stock markets to consider too. Investors in Britain thought they were doing well in 1985, when the average share quoted on the London Stock Exchange rose by 19 per cent. Take a look at this league table, adjusted for currency movements, of stock market performances in the 12 months to end-March 1987 among the world's major industrialised countries.

Table 4

		%
1	Singapore	+103
2	Japan	+ 83
3	Hong Kong	+ 66
4	New Zealand	+ 61
5	France	+ 46
6	Australia	+ 45
7	Canada	+ 34
8	UK	+ 33
9	USA	+ 19
10	West Germany	+ 12

Britain is almost bottom of the league. And going to more exotic countries (generally not to be advised), you could have done even better. The Bombay Stock Market, for example, beat even Singapore by a substantial margin.

The currency factor

If you are still feeling pleased with yourself for investing in British shares, read on. In 1985 the pound sterling fell against the Italian lira, the German deutschmark and the Swiss franc. The gains in sterling were even larger than this table suggests.

The currency factor is important from another angle. This goes back to the spread of risk covered in earlier chapters. Most British people earn their salaries in sterling, own a house giving an investment in property in sterling, hold building society deposits and National Savings Certificates in sterling, and buy shares on the British stock market denominated in, yes, you guessed it, sterling. Any spread of risk between property, fixed interest, equities, and various kinds of equities on the London Stock Exchange still leaves one major exposure – to the British currency and the British economy. The need to spread risk alone dictates that anyone with a decent level of savings should consider investing overseas in some form or other. You feel you have not suffered from exposure to the British economy? Well, fifteen years ago there were eleven Swiss francs to every pound. Now there are less than three.

From the fixed interest viewpoint, roll-up currency funds offer the easiest and cheapest way to obtain a currency spread. From the equity viewpoint, or from the viewpoint of investing in the chemical industry but choosing a share other than ICI, there are few problems.

Most of the world's leading companies have a share quote on the London Stock Exchange, that is, if they have a share quote anywhere at all. The listing at the end of this chapter gives an example of the choice available. Any stockbroker, down to the smallest two partner county firm, will be able to buy these for you. There may be a little price discrepancy between the price you would have paid if, for instance, you had bought BASF shares on the Frankfurt Stock Exchange rather than the London one, but it will not be significant because if there was a difference worth measuring the professional fund managers would take advantage of it, buying shares in Frankfurt and selling them (say) in London making an easy profit until the weight of their business forced prices to equalise. This happens all the time, and it is your guarantee against being ripped off by dealing in the London market, rather than the local one.

Going international – the easy way

Table 5 shows just a handful of major foreign companies whose shares are quoted in London. Buying in London avoids many of the administrative and taxation problems which buying on a foreign stock market produces. However, buying in London will not get you over the problem of dividends being taxed at source.

Table 5 Major world companies and their country of origin

Company	Country	Industry
Akzo	Netherlands	Chemicals
Alexander & Alexander	USA	Insurance broking
Allianz	West Germany	Insurance underwriting
Anheuser Beusch	USA	Beer
ATT	USA	Communications
Bank America	USA	Banking
Bank Leumi	Israel	Banking
Bayer	West Germany	Chemicals
Bethlehem Steel	USA	Steel
Campbells Soup	USA	Food
Chase Manhatten	USA	Banking
Citicorp	USA	Banking
Colgate Palmolive	USA	Toiletries
Commerzbank	West Germany	Banking
Copenhagen Handelsbank	Denmark	Banking
Electrolux	Sweden	Household goods
Emhart	USA	Industrial
Ford Motor	USA	Cars
General Electric	USA	Industrial
General Motors	USA	Cars
Hoechst	West Germany	Chemicals
Honda Motor	Japan	Cars
Hong Kong Land	Hong Kong	Property
Hong Kong & Shanghai Bank	Hong Kong	Banking
Hudsons Bay	Canada	Trading
Hutchinson-Whampoa	Hong Kong	Trading
IBM	USA	Computer
Marsh & McLennan	USA	Stockbroking
Nabisco	USA	Food
Norsk Hydro	Norway	Oil
Ogilvy & Mather	USA	Advertising
Philips Lamps	Netherlands	Electrical
Quaker Oats	USA	Food
Snia Viscosa	Italy	Textiles
SKF	Sweden	Ball bearings

Table 5—cont.

Company	Country	Industry
Takeda	Japan	Chemicals
TDK	Japan	Industrial
Toronto Dominion Bank	Canada	Banking
Trans Canada Pipeline	Canada	Pipelines
Union Carbide	USA	Chemicals
USX	USA	Steel
Wells Fargo	USA	Banking
Woolworth US	USA	Stores

The disadvantages

Are there disadvantages to buying foreign company shares? The simple answer is yes. In many countries, dividends are taxed at source but you will still have to pay tax on that dividend when it gets into your hands. Therefore the dividend will be taxed twice, and while it is possible to avoid getting hurt too badly under Double Taxation agreements operated by the Inland Revenue with many countries, often the shareholder in Britain will end up with a slightly smaller net dividend than an investor who lives in that country. This, of course, has no impact on capital values because the value of the share is usually determined by demand locally and is judged accordingly on the yield. There are other problems for people wishing to invest overseas. Some countries have strict controls on the number of shares in a company that foreigners may own, for example, Japan and Norway. In these countries you may find yourself paying rather more for a share in a company than a 'local' would. You are having to buy shares that are free for foreign investment when there is a shortage of them, in turn this forces up the price creating a two-tier market. Again, as long as foreign demand is firm, it is possible to view purchases here as having limited risk.

In some foreign markets, dealing in size can be difficult. This will not normally be a problem for the private investor. A far greater problem is to avoid getting stuck with the 'recommendation of the day' that many foreign stock-broking companies churn out, inundating investors with shares they want to get rid of rather than ones that are particularly good value. In investment, it is a fairly sound axiom that you cannot trust anyone. But it is probably also true that you can trust the average British stockbroker more than stockbrokers from some other countries.

If the stock in which you want to deal is not quoted on the London market, it is possible, with very little trouble, to deal on overseas stock markets. All the big stockbroking firms now have facilities to do this having established trading links with overseas banks and stockbroking organisations. Most big British stockbrokers also have teams of researchers and dealers hunting for information on foreign companies, trying to judge which companies offer the best investment opportunity from the British viewpoint. And many small firms of regional stockbrokers have links with large London ones, this way gaining access to the big brokers' foreign research.

But what is it all going the cost?

Dealing costs, conditions of settlement and local taxes vary from country to country. Be careful to check them out before dealing. Here is a brief summary of the conditions in some of the leading overseas markets.

Australia
Commission: 2.5 per cent on first A$5,000,
2.0 per cent on next A$10,000,
1.5 per cent on next A$35,000.
Half commission on a closing sale within one month of the purchase.
Stamp duty: 0.3 per cent.
Withholding tax: 30 per cent halved by Double Taxation Relief (DTR) agreements.
Settlement: Delivery of shares can take over a month, but you have to pay immediately.

Belgium
Commission: 1.0 per cent on under BFr2 million,
0.9 per cent on under BFr5 million.
Stamp duty: 0.375 per cent.
There is a fixed standing charge of BFr100 per bargain in addition to this.
Withholding tax: 25 per cent, but a full refund under DTR agreement.
Settlement: An account system similar to the UK.

Canada
Commission: Negotiable, but similar to US (see below).
Withholding tax: 25 per cent, cut to 15 per cent under DTR, sometimes more.
Settlement: After 5 days.

Denmark
Commission: 0.5 per cent if under DKR100,000. More if the share is trading below par value.
Stamp duty: 0.25 per cent.
Withholding tax: 25 per cent, reduced to 15 per cent by DTR.

France
Commission: 0.65 per cent if under FFr600,000. Extra 0.6 per cent on 'odd lot' bargains in small numbers.
Stamp duty: 0.3 per cent. VAT also at 17.5 per cent of commission for private buyers.
Withholding tax: Very complicated. Basically 25 per cent, reducing to either 15 per cent or 5 per cent with DTR.
Settlement: A monthly account system.

Germany (W)
Commission: 0.5 per cent plus 0.1 per cent brokerage.
Stamp duty: None.
Settlement: Two days after purchase.
Withholding tax: You miss a 56 per cent tax credit the Germans get locally. This puts the British investor at a disadvantage in West Germany more so than in any other market. Also, there is 25 per cent withholding tax, reduced to 15 per cent by DTR.

Hong Kong
Commission: Negotiable, but usually under 1 per cent.
Stamp duty: 3 per cent plus, and there are other taxes.
Settlement: Within 24 hours.
Withholding tax: None.

Italy
Commission: 0.7 per cent with a high minimum.
Stamp duty: 0.225 per cent.
Withholding tax: 30 per cent, but back to 15 per cent with DTR.
Settlement: Monthly account, like France.

Japan
Commission: 1.25 per cent plus a fixed charge, under Y1 million.
Stamp duty: 0.55 per cent.
Withholding tax: 20 per cent, cut to 15 per cent by DTR.
Settlement: 3 days.

Netherlands
Commission: 1.5 per cent under FLS5,000,
1.0 per cent under FLS20,000,
Plus FLS7.50.
Sometimes discounts apply.
Stamp duty: None.
Withholding tax: 25 per cent, cut to 15 per cent with DTR.
Settlement: 3 days.

Singapore
Commission: 1 per cent.
Stamp duty: 0.35 per cent, via 3 separate charges.
Withholding tax: 40 per cent, no DTR.
Settlement: Next day.

Switzerland
Commission: 1 per cent (less for shares over SF150 each).
Stamp duty: 0.9 per cent via two sources.
Withholding tax: 35 per cent, reducing to 15 per cent with DTR.
Settlement: Next day.

USA
Commission: Negotiable, averaging 1.5 per cent for the private buyer.
Stamp duty: 0.003 per cent on sales only.
Settlement: 5 days.
Withholding tax: 15 per cent under a DTR treaty.

It can be seen from this that some foreign markets present difficulties for the private individual, for example, Germany with its penal dividend export policy, and Hong Kong with its heavy stamp duty.

United Kingdom unit trusts and investment trusts specialising in particular countries can ease the problem of investing overseas, as they give a wide spread of investments and reduce the exposure to any one particular industry or share. Because they are not buying and selling shares every time their units – or in the case of investment trusts, shares – change hands, they can be a cheaper way into some markets.

6 THE MEAT OF THE MATTER – HOW PROFESSIONALS ANALYSE SHARES

How can we tell a good share from a bad one? To do this, at the very least we have to be aware of the way the professional fund managers analyse shares, so we can compare them using their yardsticks, even if we do not use this as our means of judging whether a share is good value or not. Time and time again, however, analysis comes down to this; the investor is either trying to obtain or deduce information that will give him the inside track, to know what is likely to happen ahead of the other operators in the stock market.

Insider trading is, of course, against the law. The regulations used to be so poorly framed that even for the most clumsy crook this was a matter of academic interest. New laws introduced in 1986 have changed that, and if you buy or sell shares on information you have come by illegally, you can and probably will go to jail. But there is a world of difference between being the director of a public company about to report higher profits and buying shares in the market, and calculating as an outsider by careful observation that profits will be higher, and buying shares with the benefit of that knowledge.

This is precisely how investment analysis started in America in the nineteenth century. Charles Dow, a young stockbroker, made a practice of standing outside steel mills and counting the number of chimneys belching smoke. From this he was able to tell which steel companies were prospering, and which were short of business. It kept him one step ahead of other less enterprising investors, and he grew rich on the results. He ended up founding the *Wall*

Street Journal and putting his name to that grand old US stock market indicator, the Dow Jones Index.

There are not so many quoted companies these days that have rows of chimneys belching smoke into the atmosphere, but there is still no substitute for this type of information. That means if you know someone who works for a company, even someone on the shop floor who can just tell you whether there is overtime working or short time working, if you know one of the company's suppliers, customers or competitors, then you have an advantage, and one which you should be able to put to good use.

Inside trading applies only when you are told, by someone who is obviously going to have accurate inside knowledge, what a company's profits are going to be for a year that has already finished, or if you gain certain accurate information (rather than just a rumour) of a coming takeover bid.

Industry statistics, published by trade associations, and by the Government (notably in the *Monthly Digest of Statistics* and the *Business Monitor* series of booklets, both available at good libraries) are also a great help. These statistics are, of course, historic. They do not tell much about future trends. However, if an industry has been in a consistent state of decline over the years, or growing slower than the national average, then it is going to take something pretty dramatic to change that trend. The range and diversity of these statistics is quite astonishing. If you want details of the proportion of the shoe market in this country that is being taken by imports, or the sales of vegetables that are frozen rather than sold fresh or canned, the figures are there.

Until the very early years of this century, both in the US and in Britain, information published in company profit and loss accounts was very skimpy. The word 'profit' was more or less meaningless because it was interpreted in so many different ways, what mattered was the dividend a company was likely to pay. This, for all the fact that we can rely much more on a published profit figure these days, remains the core of investment analysis. When an investor buys a share, he is laying out cash on an investment and

MAKE MORE OF YOUR MONEY

Everyone needs help when it comes to savings and investments. From the first steps into unit trusts, through 'blue chip' share advice, to some of the hottest stock market tips worldwide, *What Investment* will keep you one move ahead. Easy to read, this monthly magazine gives regular coverage to news and views that will affect your investments and presents you with simple guides as to how to make the most of your money.

There are also sections given over to comparisons of interest rates from different savings schemes and full performance details of all authorised unit trusts. And there's a free readers' enquiry service.

If you want to know how to get your copy every month, write to What Investment Subscriptions, 26 Queensway, London W2 3RX.

For the resident abroad, Financial Magazines has successfully introduced *Investment International,* the financial magazine for the British expatriate. Presented in a bright and colourful style, *Investment International* is essential reading for those who wish to take advantage of their opportunity to invest in offshore and tax-free investment vehicles. For further details contact Investment International Subscriptions, Consort House, 26 Queensway, London W2 3RX.

expects a return on that investment. The return comes as a dividend, or as capital gain which is really nothing more than other investors buying the shares in expectation of greatly increased future dividends. The newspaper comments you read, and the research sent to you by your stockbroker, will lay great emphasis upon profits and earnings per share, but really, the dividend is the only link between a share price and its profits. After tax profit is the company's dividend paying ability – or should be. Dividends are the basic roots of stock market analysis, and it is important to start with them.

The example on page 99 shows something unusual about a company's dividend payment – it is put in the profit and loss account *after* the corporation tax charge. But it would be wrong to assume from this that companies cannot offset their dividend payments against corporation tax. By and large they can. The taxation of dividends is very complicated, and is central to the way we analyse them.

The dividend a company pays to its investors appears in the accounts at a so-called 'net' figure and usually represents the actual cost to the company of paying it. When it is received by the investor, the dividend includes a tax credit on the assumption that the investor will be paying tax at the standard rate of 30 per cent on his dividend. The gross cheque received will have to be declared in the annual tax return, and will be taxed in the same way as income from any other source. That means net of tax, it will be worth only the original 'net' figure to you, or even less if you are in a high tax bracket. This enables you to compare a company's dividend yield with the yield of other fixed interest investments. Some of these, like gilt-edged stocks, are quoted 'gross'. Others, like building society deposits, are quoted net. Make sure you are comparing like with like.

It would be unfair, of course, if the company were paying its dividend out of net, taxed income, but then the investor was paying personal income tax on his dividend once he received it. Fairness is one of the abiding principles of taxation, and the current tax system makes a broad, but rather ham-fisted, attempt at it. Companies are allowed to deduct the tax credit paid to the investor, in other words, the difference between the net and gross payment from their UK corporation tax payments. Obviously, this very much reduces the total cost of a dividend for a company paying UK corporation tax. Other companies are not so lucky.

There may be many reasons why a company is not paying UK corporation tax. Most of its profits might be earned overseas. Indeed it could be paying heavy sums of tax to overseas Governments, but little or nothing in UK corporation tax. It might have made losses in past years, and be able to offset these losses against its current profits. It might be declaring profits that are not in fact recognised as profits by the Inland Revenue. Leasing companies are a classic example of this. It stands to reason, therefore, that it is wrong to expect a handsome dividend payment from a company paying little or no UK corporation tax. This applies no matter how well off the company is for cash, or how well it is trading. This is a point worth remembering. Time and time again, the stock market will give a less favourable rating to a company in this position.

This net and gross tax position is complicated, but there is a handy little trick to help work out how much in the way of dividend you are going to get for your money. Take the expected net dividend per share and divide it by 0.73. This gives you the gross dividend that the company will pay you. The Inland Revenue will take the gross figure and tax that at 27 per cent. Divide the outcome by the share price to work out gross yield. This can be compared with the yield on other shares, gilt-edged stocks, etc. But note that, when looking at yields in the past, the net dividend must be grossed up by the standard tax rate in force when the dividend was declared.

Example
Camford Engineering. Net dividend for the year 2.50p a share. Share price 140p.

$2.50 \div 0.73 = 3.42p$
$3.42 \div 140 = 2.4 \text{ per cent}$

Reverse yield gap

The yield on shares bought on the stock market is, in almost all cases, less than the yield obtained on fixed interest investments. In general, companies increase their dividends every year, while the interest on money placed in fixed interest investment is, by definition, static. As dividends are increased, year after year (investors hope), after a certain period of time the yield on shares purchased in the past will grow to equal, and then exceed, the yield on fixed interest investments.

Before measuring yields on shares and yields on fixed interest stocks, however, we have to agree their definitions. The All-Share Index represents the closest available approximation to both the stock market and the economy as a whole. The FT Industrial Index, for example, excludes all financial shares, and is biased towards the manufacturing dinosaurs of yesteryear. As for gilts, some people use Consuls, others War Loan. But the average individual (and the average institution) is far more likely to view a long-dated gilt as the alternative to equities.

The *Financial Times* quotes a whole range of different gilt indices. There are three long gilts, low-coupon, medium-coupon and high-coupon. Low-coupon shares are issued to appeal to the higher rate taxpayer and yields are distorted by tax considerations. High coupon stocks at present can entail taking a reduction in capital as the stock moves towards redemption, yet another distorting factor (see Chapter 7). That leaves the Medium-Coupon Gilt Index. Take the longest timescale, the index for gilts with a 25-year life. If, as in the facsimile on page 108, the yield here is 9.5 per cent, and the yield on the All-Share Index is 3.4 per cent, then the reverse yield gap is 6.1 per cent. Equities are yielding rather less than half of gilts, and the market is apparently looking some way forward.

The precise size of the gap varies considerably. In 1980, gilt yields were standing at 12 per cent, equity yields at 8 per cent, giving a reverse yield gap of 4 per cent. In early 1975, for one brief, terrifying moment after the failure of Burmah Oil, gilt yields were 15 per cent, equity yields 13 per cent, giving a reverse yield gap of 2 per cent. Still further into the past, before 1958, the yield on equities was usually higher than the yield on gilts. This was caused partly because both interest rates and inflation rates were very low, therefore average dividend rises were very, very low. This was partly caused because professional fund managers viewed equities as too risky an investment vehicle to pay a premium on gilts. The last part shows just how prone to swings of fashion the professional investment market is. Suggest to the average fund manager in 1958 that the average yield on equities should be less than half the average yield on gilts, and you would have been treated as eccentric, to say the least.

There are other calculations that can be made with these two figures. It is possible to take the equity yield, estimate a likely rate of growth of dividends into the future, and see how many years it will take before a purchase of equities at current levels yields the same as a purchase of gilts. With the figures in the facsimile on page 108, assuming a 15 per cent increase in the average dividend for the next two years (because companies are flush with cash) and 10 per cent thereafter (as the inflation rate will be low, say, and Britain's growth rate will be slowing down by then – you pick the criteria), it will take just under 10 years before the yields are equal. Taking a flat 10 per cent growth rate, it takes just under 11 years. If you are cautious enough to think that dividends will grow no faster than the current 4 per cent inflation rate in future, then as an investor you will be looking forward 23 years. In which time of course, you will have missed out an extra interest payments from the gilt stock that would have equalled your original capital investment. We could all be dead, as well, but that is another problem and something financial analysis can do nothing about.

Number of shares

The dividend figure is always given by companies on a 'per share' basis. Profits and earnings, particularly your profits projections, will not be available on this basis. To get them, you will have to divide your expected after-tax profits by the number of shares in issue.

Start with the consolidated balance sheet. Under the heading 'capital and reserves', the section 'called up share capital' will refer you to a note in the small print at the back of the accounts. This will give the money value of shares, both 'authorised' and 'issued'. Take the 'issued' figure. Check the listing for ordinary shares. Now find the par value of the shares. This bears no relation to the actual share price – it can be more or it can be less. You will find the phrase, 'ordinary shares of 20p each' or some other similar wording. If the par value is 20p, as in this example, then there are five shares to every £1, and if there are ordinary shares to the value of £10 million, then you have 50 million shares in issue.

Why are they called 'ordinary shares'? This is because some companies have issued financial instruments called 'preference shares'. To call these shares at all is misleading because in almost all cases their dividend is fixed, they are more of a loan stock than a share – if the company goes bankrupt, they get paid back after the loan stock holders and other creditors, although before the ordinary share-holders who, of course, come last of all. These preference shares for the most part can be ignored. There are exceptions, however. Some preference shares, and some loan stocks, can be converted into ordinary shares. It is as well to check to make sure that none of these apply to your company. Check the 'capital and reserves' section in the notes to the accounts, also the two notes to the accounts headed 'creditors', for any mention of the word 'convertible'. If it appears, you have a complication. You must now root out the conversion terms, find out how many shares the total loan stock or preference shares can be converted into, and add them to your total. With some companies you might find that the conversion terms are so far ahead of the share price, and have so little time left to run, that the convertible can be ignored completely. But this is rare.

Watch out for other types of shares as well – you might find deferred shares. A prize example of a company with these was the USM-quoted recruitment agency Hoggett

Bowers, where one of the founders left the company shortly before its flotation. His shares did not get a vote until 1989, but are otherwise identical to the ordinary shares. Those deferred shares more than doubled the total number of shares in issue, and to miss them out of your calculations would have been a grave error. Fortunately, Hoggett Bowers saved all investors the trouble of keeping track of this strange situation by allowing themselves to be taken over in the mid-1980s by Blue Arrow. Other shares that you might find include 'ordinary shares' and 'A' shares, the only difference being that one gets a vote and one does not. It is important to know this if you are thinking of buying the shares: obviously, if a takeover bid comes along the ordinary shares will be worth more. But for all your calculations, all shares in issue must be added together. 'A' shares and 'B' shares, 'participating' shares and 'restricted' shares, there are any number of names for different versions of the same thing.

Executive share option schemes are another source of extra shares, and if the company is trading well these must be counted in too. Usually, you will find they account for less than 10 per cent of the total number of shares around, or likely to be around, and would not upset your calculations unduly.

What happens when the company makes a takeover bid after the year end? Look in the Chairman's Statement or the Directors' Report as it should be noted in either place. If it has happened after the Annual Report has been issued, it will appear either on the Macarthy press cutting service or the Extel card (see Appendix) at your local library. If the takeover has been made in exchange for an issue of shares, you will have to take those shares into account in your calculations. Companies do this in one of two ways. The first is by taking an average of the number of shares in issue throughout the year and at the same time taking in only the profits earned from the time the acquisition has been made. The second is by taking the total, in which case a full twelve months' profits will be included. We will go into this later on but, for the time being, just be aware of the two different methods: you should also be aware that the averaged basis, glorified by the term 'acquisition accounting' as against 'merger accounting', for the totalling method, is strictly transitory. The year after that acquisition, the number of shares in issue will have grown correspondingly to the full number.

The same arguments apply for a rights issue – when a company has asked its shareholders to buy more shares, usually more cheaply than on the stock market. For what to do when a company you invest in has a rights issue, see Chapter 7. Some companies also confuse attempts at analysis by issuing new shares free: these are called a 'scrip issue' or a 'capitalisation issue'. These make no difference at all to the running of the company but might cause you to under-calculate the number of shares in issue. There are a few companies, happily very few, that insist on issuing some new shares along with the dividend every year.

Confused? You should not be once you try following the logic of this through on a real company's annual report. If you are unsure of how many shares there are in issue after all that, it is quite in order to telephone the company secretary, or if it is a large company someone in his department, and clarify just how many shares the company secretary thinks there are in issue. This is not inside information, and companies should (and usually are) happy to answer this question at any time, even if the annual results are due to be announced the next day. There is nothing to be ashamed about in doing so – professional investors do it all the time.

'Per share' – two key calculations

Now you know how many shares there are in issue, you can use this to calculate two key statistics. These are 'earnings per share' and 'assets per share'. Earnings per share is simply the after-tax profits, incidentally also after minority interest payments, preference dividend payments and anything else there may be, divided by the number of shares in issue. So, for example, if a company's profit and loss account shows profits after tax of £1 million, there are no preference dividends or minority interests, and there are 5 million shares in issue, then the earnings per share are £1 million divided by 5 million which equals 20p.

This calculation is a useful one for spotting companies run by directors who are more interested in building their own personal empires than making money for their investors. By making takeovers, through issuing new shares, directors can easily make pre-tax profits soar. But all too often in these cases, while pre-tax profits rise, earnings per share show only pedestrian growth, or are static. Calculating earnings per share, and working out likely earnings per share figures for future years, will help you steer clear of these boardroom megalomaniacs. It will also give you a much clearer idea of just how fast the company is growing.

The second calculation, assets per share, is particularly useful if there is the possibility of your company being faced with a takeover bid. At the time of writing, this appears to be a popular pastime. It is a rare takeover bid that is made for less than the asset backing per share – after all, it would be more profitable for the shareholders just to sell all the assets and distribute the cash than to accept a cheaper bid. If a company has a valuable property asset, this can be a useful tool to calculate how much your company is really worth, rather than what might be revealed in the balance sheet.

Assets per share are calculated by going back to the consolidated balance sheet, and totalling the items under the 'capital and reserves' heading, sometimes entitled 'shareholders funds'. If there are preference shares in issue, then you will have to deduct their value from the total. You will find this in the notes to the accounts. You also will have to make an adjustment if there are subsidiaries partly owned by the parent company but whose figures are included in your total. Divide the figure you are left with by the number of shares in issue. For example, if a company has a total of capital and reserves of £50 million, but has £3 million of preference shares in issue, and 12 million ordinary shares in issue, then its assets per share are:

$$\frac{£50m - £3m}{12m} = \frac{£47m}{12m} = 391p$$

If the company has a valuable property, find out its value as noted in the accounts. Is this a fair value, or could the property be worth more? Do read the accounts as they will contain some clues. If not, ring up and ask the company secretary. Replace the company's book figure with the figure you think is the true value of the property, and do the sum all over again.

The price/earnings ratio

Now you have calculated an earnings per share figure, divide it into the share price to give a 'price/earnings' ratio (p/e ratio). For the last 15 years this has been the vogue ratio to use for investment analysis, indeed to hear the fuss made about it you would think there were not any other ratios. In terms of assessing what a company is actually worth, as a ratio it is somewhat flawed, but even so, it is a useful assessment as share values are decided by people *who think* the shares are worth a lot rather than by the actual value at the time; certainly this is applicable to the short-term valuation. Therefore, we are going to have to treat the p/e ratio with the same kind of awe and respect that it gets elsewhere in the investment community.

The p/e ratio started out life as a sophisticated indicator of whether a company was likely to produce a dramatic increase in its dividend. In theory, if a company was paying a small dividend but earning large profits, it just *might* announce a big dividend increase at some future time, pushing up the yield and therefore creating a rise in the share price. Even if the dividend were not increased, then the money was being stacked aside under 'capital and reserves' where it rightly belonged to shareholders, and the more money that accumulated there, the higher assets per share rose. However, life was not always that simple. Sometimes high inflation made a mockery of published profits figures, and companies physically could not pay out all their profits in dividends because of the need to finance the cost of increasing stock levels. Sometimes companies paid out dividends far higher than their annual earnings in order to keep their share price up. But by and large the theory on p/e ratios worked often enough for it to be adopted with enthusiasm by the investment community.

Since then the statistics have been distorted somewhat by the introduction of the imputation system of corporation tax that we described on page 99, but the logic holds the same.

How do you use a p/e ratio? Generally speaking, the higher the ratio, the faster the rate of growth the stock market is expecting in the future. But to use this ratio properly, you need to know not only the ratio for the company in which you are thinking of investing, but also some comparable ratios. These can be found four pages or so from the back of the *Financial Times*, under the heading 'Financial Times Actuaries Indices' (see page 108).

Here you will find a p/e ratio for the average industrial share, and if you want to be even more precise (as indeed you might), a whole host of p/e ratios for the average builders merchant, the average mechanical engineer, the average brewer, etc. Unfortunately, this useful table does not extend itself to giving average p/e ratios for service industry companies such as banks and insurance brokers – although all investment analysts at stockbroking firms calculate them – here you are on your own.

If the p/e ratio on the company you are analysing is lower than the comparable p/e ratio in this table, then it could be that the stock market expects your company to grow at a slower rate than the average. But you might know something the stock market does not know! Indeed that should be your central aim, and if you believe your company is going to raise its earnings per share faster than the average, then you may have a bargain on your hands.

Some companies are in such esoteric industries that to look for any direct comparison among these indices is pretty meaningless. With these, the best thing is to analyse some comparable individual companies, so you can see which is best value – or as a short cut – take the p/e ratios printed for comparable companies in the daily newspapers. But this is a short cut, newspaper calculations are not always that accurate.

Table 6

FT ACTUARIES SHARE INDICES

These indices are the joint compilation of the Financial Times,
the Institute of Actuaries and the Faculty of Actuaries

EQUITY GROUPS & SUB-SECTIONS Figures in parentheses show number of stocks per section	Index No.	Gross Div Yield % (ACT at 29%)	Est. P/E Ratio (Net)	Year ago (approx) Index No.
1 CAPITAL GOODS (207)	855.22	3.13	16.92	722.20
2 Building Materials (27)	1065.91	3.11	17.13	823.59
10 Other Industrial Materials (20)	1458.46	3.43	19.61	1305.74
21 CONSUMER GROUP (188)	1157.10	2.81	20.30	943.57
a · 22 Brewers and Distillers (22)	1058.89	3.28	15.59	944.53 · b
25 Food Manufacturing (26)	877.99	3.46	17.26	688.58
40 OTHER GROUPS (88)	980.29	3.50	15.49	843.96
42 Chemicals (21)	1223.53	3.61	15.43	906.21
45 Shipping and Transport (11)	1988.13	4.09	17.94	1660.51
c · 47 Telephone Networks (2)	987.31	3.90	14.40	1027.18
48 Miscellaneous (25)	1354.08	3.32	12.65	1026.75
49 INDUSTRIAL GROUP (483)	1043.91	3.08	17.89	870.39 · d
51 Oil & Gas (17)	1873.95	4.75	13.98	1183.19
71 Investment Trusts (95)	974.71	2.43	—	749.60
81 Mining Finance (2)	437.98	3.75	16.81	315.12
g-e · 91 Overseas Traders (11)	901.14	4.99	13.38	695.27 · d-f
99 ALL-SHARE INDEX (725)	1000.04	3.45	—	818.36

h · AVERAGE GROSS REDEMPTION YIELDS		Tues March 31	Mon March 30	Year ago (approx.)
British Government				
i · 1 Low	5 years	8.17	8.14	8.03
2 Coupons	15 years	9.04	9.14	8.45
3	25 years	9.06	9.16	8.46
4 Medium	5 years	9.13	9.18	8.94
5 Coupons	15 years	9.21	9.32	8.80
j · 6	25 years	9.22	9.32	8.77
7 High	5 years	9.24	9.29	9.03
8 Coupons	15 years	9.35	9.43	8.95
9	25 years	9.16	9.24	8.88
k · 10 Irredeemables		9.05	9.12	8.57

Source: *The Financial Times.* From the issue dated, Wednesday April 1st, 1987.

Table 6 – FT Actuaries Share Indices – an explanation.

(a) If you are thinking of buying shares in Whitbread, compare it to this.

(b) Average brewery share up by 12 per cent in 12 months. Only half the rate of the market average, which rose 22 per cent! This means, do not bother to compare British Telecom with this. British Telecom *is* the index!

(c) Sadly, no p/e ratio for the All-Share Index, use the Industrial Index instead.

(d) This shows the 'average yield'. How does your investment compare with it?

(e) The average share has risen by 22 per cent in the last 12 months.

(f) The All-Share Index is the nearest thing to the 'average' share.

(g) This heading means not just your six monthly dividend cheque, but also the average change in value as the stock moves up (or down) towards its repayment price (usually £100).

(h) Good investment if you are a top rate taxpayer. Most of the 'yield' is capital gain.

(i) Most accurate for calculating the reverse yield gap.

(j) Some of these are paid tax-free – good if you do not pay any tax.

As you become really professional at investment, you will be doing these calculations on *future* earnings, rather than past ones. After all, the earnings for the year just past will pretty soon be consigned to the dustbin of history. And here, your newspaper gets less and less useful.

What influences profits?

Every company has certain factors it is vulnerable to, and certain factors that will give it an exceptionally strong lift if things go right for it. It is important to identify these. To do this we need to draw up a profile of the major factors affecting the company's profit and loss account. Not all of these factors are shown in the one page profit and loss account that companies print in their accounts. There are some items of interest hidden in the notes at the back of the accounts. The factors of interest can be counted as follows:

– exports and overseas sales;
– pre-tax profit/sales margins;
– interest money in;
– interest money out;
– depreciation;
– tax.

Taking a well-known company as an example, ICI, gives us the following picture.

Table 7

Sales	£9,900m
Exports/overseas sales	£5,500m
Exports overseas as percentage = 56%	
Interest in	£90m
Interest in as percentage pre-tax profit = 29%	
Interest out	£187m
Interest out as percentage pre-tax profit = 18%	
Depreciation	£440m
Depreciation as percentage pre-tax profit = 42%	
Pre-tax profits	£1,034m
Pre-tax profits/sales = 10.4%	
Tax	£373m
Tax as percentage of pre-tax profits = 36%	

Let us take another company, Whitbread, which gives us this picture.

Table 8

Sales	£1,444m
Exports/overseas sales	£337m
Exports/overseas as percentage = 23%	
Interest in	£8.8m
Interest in as percentage pre-tax profit = 8%	
Interest out	£32m
Interest out as percentage pre-tax profit = 29%	
Depreciation	£37m
Depreciation as percentage = 33%	
Pre-tax profit	£110m
Pre-tax profit/sales margin = 7.6%	
Tax	£25m
Tax as percentage of profits = 23%	

Taking these two examples, let us analyse the items on a point-by-point basis.

Exports/overseas sales

If you believe the pound sterling is going to be strong, you have to think twice before preferring ICI to Whitbread. Whitbread's overseas exposure is 23 per cent. ICI, on the other hand, is getting 56 per cent of its sales from overseas. If sterling rises and other currencies fall, ICI will have trouble fighting off foreign competition, the money it makes from its overseas subsidiaries will be worth less when it is changed to sterling. Obviously, all other factors being equal, the risk/reward of profit and losses/gains on exports is usually greater than that from overseas manufacturing operations.

There are two further factors to watch. The first is the currencies which a company is vulnerable to. With ICI, for all its vast US interests, the deutschmark is almost as important as the dollar. This is because three out of the world's five largest chemical firms are German, and Germany has to be counted as a major competitor. Annual reports give a breakdown of both sales and profits by geographical area, therefore it is possible to obtain a detailed check on how specific exchange rate movements affect any one company.

The second factor is that companies have different methods of accounting for currency changes. Most of them take an average exchange rate for the year – a profit earned in Germany in February is translated from deutschmarks to sterling in February. Some translate all earnings from overseas operations at the year-end exchange rate, ignoring what has been happening at the time the transactions took place. Neither method is perfect from the accounting point of view, not least because the company might not have translated the profits earned on that business back to sterling at that particular time. But a company that sticks rigorously to the year-end method is capable of presenting surprises should the exchange rates change dramatically in the final month before year-end.

Some companies cover their future currency requirements in the forward currency markets. Lewmar, the yachting equipment manufacturer, was floated on the stock market in the summer of 1985. It used the forward currency markets to buy forward its currency needs for the rest of the year at an average exchange rate of US$1.30 to £1. In a year when the exchange rate had been as low as US$1.05 to £1 and was to rise as high as US$1.48 to £1, it was a great help to investors and management alike to know precisely where the company stood on currencies – particularly as 90 per cent of the company's production was either being exported or manufactured overseas.

Interest in or out

Changes in interest rates can have a dramatic effect on companies with a very high ratio of interest charges (or interest income) to pre-tax profits. This might not always be apparent from the balance sheet. A company might have relatively low borrowings in relation to capital employed, and not be in any conventional danger of going bankrupt. If the company is making very low profits, however, then a quite moderate rise in interest rates could wipe out profits. This relationship between interest charges on debt and the pre-tax profit is called 'operational gearing'. Obviously, if interest rates look like going up, you steer clear of companies with high operational gearing.

Both the companies analysed here look relatively safe from this point of view. ICI has in the past been a voracious consumer of capital. But three good years in the chemical industry coupled with some hefty axe work at unprofitable parts of the business have given ICI a good cash inflow lately. Clearly, any conceivable trend in interest rates is not going to make much difference to the company.

With Whitbread, there is a similar story. However, the company has more debt than ICI. But interest is not a problem for either company.

Other businesses are not so lucky. But when you find a company that does appear interest rate sensitive, check to make sure that there is not something in the way the business is structured that means they are able to recoup interest costs some other way. Banks and leasing companies are examples here. They tend to borrow heavily, but when interest rates rise, they are able to charge customers more. Indeed, banks end up making more profit because around a third of the money they use is provided by current account holders, who do not have to be paid any interest at all (see Chapter 9).

Depreciation

If the depreciation charge is high in relation to pre-tax profits, and the company has a large capital spending programme about to start, watch out. Higher capital spending means higher depreciation in future, so profits could drop. The whole point of capital spending, of course, is to increase profits, either by replacing old, unprofitable plant with new equipment thereby earning increased margins, or by expanding capacity by adding totally new plant. But life does not always work out according to plan. There have been cases, particularly in the chemical industry, where a new plant has been erected at vast cost, and once all the money has been spent, found not to work.

Companies with a heavy depreciation charge in relation to pre-tax profits are usually no problem when the inflation rate is low. But when the inflation rate rises, watch out. Depreciation is the writing off of equipment (and cars, lorries and buildings) over several years, after the money has actually been spent. It is *not* a reserve being created ready for new capital spending in the future. A high inflation rate means the cost of new equipment in future will rise dramatically. But the write-offs fixed on the plant being depreciated will be fixed, and will not provide nearly enough money to replace that plant when it wears out. Profits will have been *overstated*, creating a dangerously misleading picture of the company's worth and financial health. Not only would properly adjusted depreciation charges wipe out a lot of profits, but the company might have trouble finding the cash to meet its future capital spending bills.

Taking our two companies, once more, ICI depreciation is running at 42 per cent of pre-tax profits, while
Whitbread's shows 33 per cent of pre-tax profits. So, both
companies, Whitbread in particular, pass this test with
flying colours. Other companies will not. If this is the case
then you have to decide if a high inflation rate is likely over
the period which you will be holding the shares. If it is, then
steer clear and find another investment.

It is also important to check the relationship between
depreciation and capital spending. Roughly speaking, if
the annual capital spend is higher than the depreciation
charge, it would be wise to expect depreciation to rise
in future. If the annual capital spend is lower than the
depreciation charge, depreciation may well drop in future.

This begs the questions of whether anyone would want
to invest any money in a company that is investing less on
its new plant and equipment than it has spent in the past.
By the nature of things, in an inflationary environment,
capital spending ought to be rising each year, and therefore
the depreciation charge along with it. Regrettably, it has
been a weakness of managements since time immemorial to
cut back on spending in order to make profits look better
than they would otherwise be. That does not apply just to
manufacturing companies, either. Hotel chains can
squeeze a little extra profit by redecorating after eight years
instead of their usual six. But when the redecorating
bill comes in, it will be all the larger, and in the mean-
time customers will have been put off by the shoddy
surroundings.

Check to make sure the company you are planning to
invest in has been increasing its capital spending, and its
depreciation.

Margins

Conventional financial analysis teaches us that a company
with low pre-tax profit margins on sales is a poor company,
and that high margins are good because they are a sign of
efficiency and tight management.

You should be looking at the matter the other way round.

If a company is earning low pre-tax margins on sales, then quite a small increase in efficiency, or selling prices, can have a major impact on profits. If a badly managed company making 3 per cent profit on sales when all its competitors are making 6 per cent merely raises its margins to the industry average, it has doubled its profits.

There is vulnerability, of course. A price war that cuts prices by 3 per cent will wipe out this company's profits completely while those of the industry as a whole will only halve. In these circumstances there can be little doubt which company will go to the wall first. But how about the vulnerability of the company making margins of 15 per cent, or 20 per cent on sales? Which major customer, when it comes to negotiating a big contract, is going to resist the opportunity to bargain the price down? The buyer can see how much profit this company is making. Also business rivals, and companies in totally different lines of business, can see how profitable that line of work is and might be tempted to compete.

This can and does happen. Consider the sad case of Andre de Brett. This company came to the USM in 1983 and, as a private company, had built up a rewarding niche in the otherwise highly competitive mail order industry, specialising in clothes for the larger woman. Its huge margins were made public in the launch prospectus. Competitors sat up and took notice: two of them launched rival lines of mail order clothing for outsize women. Andre de Brett's sales and profits fell sharply. Andre de Brett's share price did not do too well either.

In general, if margins are high, or are higher than those of competitors, be careful. Again, a little arithmetic can show you why. A company with sales of £10 million and margins of 15 per cent will make pre-tax profits of £1.5 million. The following year sales could increase beyond the dreams of avarice, to £14 million. But if margins are squeezed to a still very healthy 10 per cent, then pre-tax profits will actually fall to £1.4 million and all that magnificent growth in sales will have been totally wasted.

Tax

Tax can have an impact on a company's earnings out of all proportion to its appearance at first sight. It can eat up profits from a company that is otherwise growing quite nicely.

Take a company with profits of £1 million, but not paying any tax. Its net earnings are therefore also £1 million. Next year its profits rise to £1.2 million. But it starts paying tax, a 20 per cent charge, which amounts to £240,000. Net earnings have now dropped to £960,000! A further year of profits growth to £1.4 million pre-tax, while the tax charge rises to a standard UK rate of 35 per cent, and tax is soaking up £490,000, leaving only £910,000 for the poor investors!

In this example, two very good years of pre-tax profits growth have been transformed to two years of falling earnings for shareholders. But if your company is allowing for only a low rate of tax, ask yourself (or the company) why, and if this is likely to last.

After all these calculations, do you still think the company you have found is a bargain? Go back and think again, this time from the point of view of someone selling the shares, or someone thinking of buying a competitor's company shares. Maybe you have not thought of everything! Maybe someone else out there knows more than you do.

When you have done all that, good luck.

7 ANALYSIS – IN MORE DETAIL

Analysing the profit and loss account is fine as far as it goes, but no investment should ever be made without a study of the 'consolidated balance sheet'. It is the consolidated balance sheet that will throw up hints on the likelihood of the company going bankrupt, or getting itself so stretched financially that its bankers will force it to stop expanding and insist that time is devoted to putting the firm on a sound financial footing.

The annual report for most companies contains *two* balance sheets. The one that is labelled 'balance sheet' will be for the PLC company in which you own shares. This is of strictly limited use: indeed, in nine cases out of ten, it is of no use whatsoever. Because a parent company holds shares in other companies, its subsidiaries, these are far more important to the overall company financial picture: but the assets and liabilities of these subsidiaries will not be reflected in the parent company's balance sheet. For the overall picture, it is the 'consolidated balance sheet' that matters. To save confusion, particularly when checking back on something in a hurry, it is usually best to run a pencil line through the parent company's balance sheet.

When looking at the money shown in the balance sheet, do not believe that it all belongs to shareholders. Some of it has been borrowed from banks, some will have been earmarked to pay bills for everything from raw materials to your dividend cheques. The amount labelled 'shareholders' funds' is what rightfully belongs to shareholders, and if the company were to be wound up tomorrow, only this amount would (items such as redundancy payments apart) find its way to you, the shareholder.

In this respect a consolidated balance sheet is very much like your own personal financial situation. As an individual, you are custodian of an impressive amount of wealth in the form of your house, investments, and wages due to you at the end of the month, right down to the food in the fridge and even the pension due to you upon your retirement. However, not all this impessive sum of wealth is yours. You are looking after some on behalf of the building society (mortgage), bank (overdraft), more banks (credit cards), the rates, the gas, the electricity . . . and the list goes on.

The figure for shareholders' funds in the consolidated balance sheet needs to be treated with a fair amount of caution. If a property is heavily undervalued, this can give a misleadingly low figure for shareholders' funds, in the same way that your total wealth as an individual would appear misleadingly low if your house was included at its purchase price rather than its present value. There are similar problems on the other side of the equation; the most important one is 'intangibles' – that is, goodwill. But what is goodwill? All businesses have some form of a goodwill element, such as loyalty built-up over years of trading with existing customers. Your company may have taken over rival businesses in the past and their company accounts will have been incorporated into your own, a goodwill element will therefore be present. So part of the business acquired by takeover will have goodwill listed, while part of it, the business core, will not. This is clearly illogical. There is another reason for ignoring it; your company might have been mismanaging its acquisitions since it made them. If it has been upsetting customers, losing orders, messing around with the product range, then the goodwill would have been dissipated, its cost elements will not be nearly as much as the price paid at acquisition, and a loss would be made if the acquired company were resold. When a bank manager is approached to lend money to your company, he will not take much notice of the 'goodwill' factor. So strip it out – deduct it from the total of shareholders' funds.

Are there any other assets listed that could be of doubtful value? The answer is yes. Goods (stock) that have passed

through the factory but have not yet been sold might be sitting in a warehouse somewhere because nobody wants them. Debtors, in other words companies who owe money to the company, might not pay up. While 'fixed assets' – i.e. factories, land, etc. – might seem safe enough, there are parts of the country where industrial property is not as valuable as it once was. And what about 'research and development' that is included in the balance sheet as an asset? In the early 1970s, this element fooled people into thinking Rolls Royce was still solvent when it was not. Since Rolls Royce, you will not find it listed as research and development, but it still pops up as experimental machinery listed as a fixed asset, or a prototype listed under stock. 'Contingent liabilities', listed under the notes at the back of the balance sheet, can be another problem. Legal actions and a host of other horrors have a habit of showing up here, and are easily missed by superficial perusal of the annual report.

So shareholders' funds are not always what they appear to be and this is why bankers are sometimes unwilling to lend a company very much money. Bankers' attitudes to a company can make a great deal of difference to the amount of profit it generates, therefore it is important to read a balance sheet in the same way as a banker does – with suspicion.

Bankers watch the total level of debt compared to shareholders' funds. As methods of preparing accounts, and valuing assets, vary from company to company and also between firms of auditors, bankers also place great emphasis on the *change* in a balance sheet from one year to the next.

To find total debt, it is necessary to delve into the notes on the accounts. Most debt is accumulated by way of short-term bank borrowings, and these only show up in the main consolidated balance sheet as part of 'short-term liabilities', most of which are relatively innocuous. To that, add any other debt that can be found, loan stocks, longer term bank borrowings, or sums due under leasing agreements. The latter is also found in the notes to the accounts and is important because a lease agreement functions in just the same way as an HP agreement or a medium-term bank loan.

From this total debt, deduct any spare cash in the bank that the company might have. Strange though it may seem, companies often have spare cash in one account and an overdraft in another. Different subsidiaries, and operations in different countries, will have their finances handled separately. But for the investor, it is the overall position that matters.

In general, a company can be described as having a low level of borrowing if its total debt amounts to below 25 per cent of shareholders' funds after stripping out goodwill, an acceptable level of gearing at between 25 per cent and 45 per cent, and a high level of gearing over 45 per cent. This is a rule of thumb rather than an immutable law; some companies trade happily year after year with debt of 60 per cent and upwards of shareholders' funds. Banks are far more likely to be disturbed by a rise in 'gearing' from 10 per cent to 40 per cent without adequate explanation than by a company with a steady gearing of 80 per cent, but which has reduced the figure from 100 per cent the year before.

Those who take this analysis really seriously go back to compare three, four and even five years' balance sheets in this way. For many companies, making takeovers or meeting changing business conditions, comparison over too long a timescale is not always easy. But nevertheless, it is a good discipline to get into. How do the sums work? Take a company with a balance sheet which looks like the one laid out in Table 9.

Table 9   Balance sheet

Fixed assets	£200
Current assets	£100
Cash in bank	–
Bank debt	£50
Other short-term liabilities	£50
Long-term loan	£60
Shareholders' funds	£140

The gearing equation is:

$$\frac{\text{Bank debt} + \text{long-term loan}}{\text{Shareholders' funds}} \quad \frac{50 + 60}{140} = \frac{100}{140} = 78 \text{ per cent}$$

While on the subject of gearing, it is worth pointing out that Continental banks pay only limited attention to this type of calculation, known technically there as 'capital' gearing. They concentrate more upon 'income' gearing, in other words, the ratio of interest charges to pre-tax profits. This method shows the ability of the company to keep up the interest payments, rather than its ability to pay back the loans. The income gearing ratio is one that needs to be given some attention because Continental banks, German banks in particular, are starting to make inroads into the British commercial lending market.

There are two other ratios that are relevant when looking at the state of a company's financial health, these are the 'current' ratio and 'acid test' ratio.

The current ratio

In the balance sheet there are two headings that can be used in relation to each other, 'current assets', and 'current liabilities' – in other words, the money due to come into the company over the next twelve months, and the money due to be paid out by the company over the next twelve months. Expressing current assets as a proportion of current liabilities gives the 'current ratio'. The larger the ratio, the healthier the state of the company. The ratio should be over 1:1, preferably 1.3:1, and should be static or rising, not falling. The direction of movement is more important than the absolute figure.

The acid test ratio

The most unreliable part of a manufacturing company's balance sheet, when it comes to the need to raise cash quickly, is the 'stock' or 'inventory' figure. The current ratio measures the company's ability to generate cash quickly, but its big weakness is that it includes stock in its cash generating assets. Not only might it take a long time to sell the stock, but it may be impossible to sell it at anything like the balance sheet valuation figure. The 'acid test' ratio sidesteps the problem by stripping the stock figure out from the calculations. The equation therefore is:

$$\frac{\text{Current assets} - \text{Stock}}{\text{Current liabilities}} = \text{Acid test ratio}$$

A desirable figure shows a ratio of more than 1:1. Less than 0.7:1 indicates a need for certain caution. Again, the figure should be either rising or static, *not* falling.

Source and application of funds

By law, PLC companies have to include in their annual accounts a table that shows where they get their money from, and how they spend it. This is called the 'source and application of funds'. The way many company accounts present this, however, could almost be calculated to confuse. It is well worth a little time and trouble to draw up your own flow of funds statement taken from the information found in the profit and loss account, the balance sheet, and the notes to the accounts. The main items to be ferreted out are shown below in Table 10. Because this is a simplified list, it may not precisely balance. If it does not balance, do not worry as long as you can identify *why* it is not balancing, and see whether there is any other area that has suddenly assumed importance in this particular case.

Table 10 helps you see several things. It may be, for example, that debt has been falling in the consolidated balance sheet. The automatic assumption is that the company has been trading more profitably, and is in a healthy state. *But* it may have reduced its debt by selling off spare land or equipment, or by curbing its capital spending figures, and this might not be repeatable in the following year. An improvement in the balance sheet might have come about because of cash brought in from a new share issue. Depreciation might be outrunning capital spending – something no manufacturing company can keep up for long without running the risk of its machinery becoming dangerously outdated.

Inventory control

When a company has a holding of stocks, or inventory, that inventory is costing money to maintain. Money is either being borrowed from banks costing interest, or is coming out of a deposit where it would have been earning interest. In addition, the higher the inventory figure, the greater the risk of the inventory becoming outdated and losing value. Only if the inventory is made up of the kind of objects that will rise in value is there any point in tying up a great deal of money here.

Inventory control is the measurement of management efficiency and is in turn measured by means of the 'stock turn' figure. This figure links the inventory figure to the total sales figure, and shows the length of time it takes the company to 'turn over' its stock. It is usually measured in days, but can also be measured in weeks.

The obvious way of doing this is to take the stock figure, divide it by the turnover figure, and multiply the result by 365 (for the number of days in the year). However, we have a distortion if we keep the sum this simple. The sales figure has been accumulated over a twelve month period. The inventory figure is a figure at *a particular moment in time* – the year-end, the balance sheet date. If the company has been growing rapidly, the business at the year-end will be very much larger than it was at the start of the year, and therefore it would be only reasonable to expect the inventory figure to be larger too. We need to know what the inventory figure was *as an average throughout the year*.

In order to build up an average, the more figures there are for the sample, the better. We do not have lots of figures, but we do have a year-start inventory figure, the figure with which the company closed off its previous financial year. This is not perfect, but is better than nothing, and in fact accountants and financial analysts alike find the resulting calculation a very useful tool.

$$\frac{(\text{Year-start stock} + \text{Year-end stock}) \times 0.5}{\text{The year's sales}} \times 365$$
$$= \text{Stock turn in days}$$

One important note relating to the above equation: it is important that the financial year being analysed is precisely twelve months. It is no good adjusting the '× 365' to another number as a balance factor if, say, the company is reporting a thirteen- or fifteen-month period because most companies carry rather more inventory at one particular time of the year than at others; and there is a great risk of seasonal factors distorting the calculation.

Table 10

In		Out
Retained earnings	OR	Retained losses
Depreciation		Capital spending
Increase in creditors (payables)		Increase in debtors (receivables)
OR		OR
Decrease in debtors (receivables)		Decrease in creditors (payables)
Reduction in stock (inventory)	OR	Increase in stock (inventory)
Income from sale of subsidiaries/land, plant and equipment		Spending on acquisition
Increase in cash		Decrease in borrowings
Increase in borrowings		Decrease in cash
Issue of new share capital		Repayment of share capital
Total in (equals roughly)		Total out

The bald figure for stock turn is no use by itself. There is no wrong figure or right figure. A firework manufacturer would be quite entitled, in mid-August, to be sitting on nine months' finished inventory. A newspaper publisher, on the other hand, who has any finished inventory (as distinct from rolls of paper and cans of ink) at all is in serious trouble. The figure is very useful, however, for comparison with the previous year's stock turn for the same company. If the figure is smaller then the company is getting more efficient. By the same token, if it is getting larger, the company could be getting less efficient.

It is also an interesting exercise to compare this figure across the same industry, but between different companies. It is particularly revealing for retailers, where comparisons between two supermarket chains, or two ladies clothing retailers, can throw up some fascinating discrepancies that interestingly tie-in showing which of the companies is making the higher profit on sales and has the faster growth rate.

As with most things, it is possible to chase the great god of stock control to absurd conclusions. A shop which does not have any goods on its shelves will not make any sales. What is more, it will alienate those unsatisfied customers who come through its doors – and those customers will find the goods they want in a rival shop, and continue to return to this new source of supply the following week and thereafter. Even so, used with just a modicum of common sense, the stock turn figure can be a very useful tool.

Receivables/payables control

The logic of these particular measures of management efficiency, and the method of calculating them, parallels that of the inventory control/stock turn figure.

The quicker a company can get money in from its customers, and the longer it can put off paying its own bills, the better its balance sheet will be, resulting in either the cash difference earning interest or the lower its borrowing figure (overdraft) can be kept. As with stock control, it is possible to take this argument to absurd levels. A customer who is being pestered to pay bills in an unrealistically short time will be alienated and take business elsewhere, while a supplier who is not paid for months on end may decide to find a new customer elsewhere or, more likely, load his prices to compensate for the late payment.

Receivables, money due in from customers, are listed in the balance sheet as debtors. The American term receivables is much clearer not only because it is self-explanatory but the term debtor sounds and looks too much like its opposite, creditors. Still, it is debtors we are stuck with.

Debtor control is measured in days, again with a year-start/ year-finish average, against sales.

$$\frac{(\text{Year-start debtors} + \text{Year-end debtors}) \times 0.5}{\text{Year's sales}}$$
$$\times\ 365 = \text{Debtor control in days}$$

Payables use precisely the same formula to calculate how long suppliers are being kept waiting for their money.

$$\frac{(\text{Year-start creditors} + \text{Year-end creditors}) \times 0.5}{\text{Year's sales}}$$
$$\times\ 365 = \text{Creditor control in days}$$

The same cautions apply about ensuring that the year is calculated as *precisely* twelve months long.

Rights issues

Every so often a quoted company will ask its shareholders for more money. When this happens, this is called a rights issue. It may seem a bit of a cheek because companies are supposed to supply their shareholders with money via dividends rather than vice versa, and until it is proven otherwise, a cheek is how you should regard it. Corps of professional fund managers encourage rights issues, firstly, because it provides the population as a whole with the only conceivable justification for putting up with a Stock Exchange at all, that of raising fresh capital for industry, and secondly, it is often the only way fund managers can get hold of enough stock to build up an economic holding in a smaller company. You, the private investor, neither need to carry the City's political worries upon your shoulders, nor have worries about accumulating a holding in sufficient stock. You are perfectly entitled to give every rights issue you meet the cold shoulder, and indeed, on the grounds that successful companies are usually generating cash rather than consuming it, there are very sound analytical reasons for doing so.

Cold shoulder rights issues but do not ignore them. Rights issues are usually made at below the ruling stock market price, and the rights themselves can be sold in the stock market for cash, the difference between the rights price and the ordinary market price for the shares. Quite often, selling the rights in the stock market raises a little more than this.

When a rights issue is made, the allotment letter for your portion flutters through your letter box and the rights start trading on the stock market; there is a period of three weeks or so before the holder of the allotment letter has to hand over the cash. In three weeks' time, however, there will be no practical difference between the old shares and the new ones. But for those three weeks, the more speculatively orientated members of the investment community have the luxury of gambling in that share while putting only part of the money up. If the price of the underlying share rises, the price of the rights also rises, proportionately far more, as shown below.

Example

Price of original share   120p
Rights issue made at   90p
Difference   30p (and therefore theoretical
                               price of rights)

But if the price of the underlying share rises by 30p to 150p. Percentage rise from 120p to 150p:

$$\frac{150 - 120}{120} \times 100 = 25 \text{ per cent}$$

Price of nil paid rights also rises by 30p, to 60p. Percentage rise from 30p to 60p:

$$\frac{60 - 30}{30} \times 100 = 100 \text{ per cent}$$

These rights, called 'nil paid rights', have attractions for other investment players too. Potential bidders intent on building up a strategic share stake can do so easily because large numbers of potential votes are washing around and can be picked up while generating relatively little attention. Also, there is a safety first element involved; if the price of the underlying share falls from 120p to 60p, there is a price fall of 60p, but the rights issue will merely have become worthless, only falling by their original 30p. (Note, however, that the loss in the rights is 100 per cent, but in the underlying shares merely 50 per cent. If you invest as much money in the rights as you intended to invest in the underlying shares you will lose badly on this basis.)

Those nil paid rights, with a theoretical value of 30p, might trade on the stock market at 33p or even 35p. Selling the nil paid rights in the market rather than taking up the shares you have been offered could net you a bit of extra profit.

If you completely ignore the rights issue, the company will usually sell the rights on your behalf and send you a cheque for the proceeds. However, that only applies in Britain; on overseas stock markets it does not always happen, and even in Britain it is not foolproof. Anyway, do you want to be dependent upon someone else to produce the money that is rightfully yours?

In throwing a rights issue, a company will alter the level of its share price. As the new shares are being issued at a cheaper price, once the rights are trading nil paid, the price for the underlying shares will readjust at a weighted average between the two.

Share originally trading at 350p
One for three rights issue made at 280p
New theoretical price: $\dfrac{350 + 350 + 350 + 380}{4} = 332.5p$

In this particular case, as a shareholder, you would be wrong to have expected the rights to start trading in nil paid form on the stock market at 70p premium. The rights theoretical price is *not* the current original share price before rights (i.e. 350p) *less* its rights offer price (280p), *but* its new theoretical price (332.5p) *less* the rights offer price (280p). In other words 332.5p − 280p = 52.5p.

A rights issue will also disturb your careful calculations about current year earnings per share. Profits ought to go up because the company will be either saving interest charges or earning extra investment interest upon the cash it is raising. But the number of shares to be divided into the after-tax profits will be greater. If the company is producing a return higher than the interest savings generated by the extra cash, its earnings per share will fall until the new money can be put to use in new machine tools, an acquisition, or whatever.

If the company has a return on capital lower than the interest savings generated by the new money, its earnings per share will rise. In that case, of course, you might be justified in asking why the company is asking for more cash, and what will happen when it finds a proper use for the cash, earning presumably a lower return than the savings it is generating in overdraft interest!

A rights issue will have an astonishing effect upon a company's balance sheet, knocking your worries about the high level of gearing for a six. Consider this example.

	£
Shareholders' funds	200
Total debt	300
Gearing	150 per cent

Verdict: Company financially unsafe.

The company, however, manages to persuade its shareholders to fund a rights issue thereby increasing the share capital by 50 per cent. This raises shareholders funds by £100, and reduces the debt by £100. Therefore the new position is:

	£
Shareholders' funds	300
Total debt	200
Gearing	67 per cent

Verdict: Financial position dramatically improved – worth considering as an investment.

Very occasionally, a company will raise a rights issue at a *higher* price than the underlying share price. This is fascinating as it usually indicates that someone is underwriting the rights issue, deliberately placing a high level on it in the hope that other shareholders will ignore this expensive offer; if he or she has planned correctly then controlling interest or a strategically important stake in the company will have been bought. The new investor is unlikely to put extra cash into the company at above the market price without doing something to make sure that the company's prospects are much improved. This is often the sign that the share is one to follow.

Watch out for rights issues made in the form of Convertible Loan Stock. If the company does badly, its profits as well as its share price fall – this means that the company will be stuck servicing extra debt. If the company does well, the profits and the share price will rise. The loan stock will be converted into shares, and the company will have a larger number of shares which will be staking a claim to its profits, thus diluting earnings per share.

Convertible loan stock is an awkward way for a company to raise money because the holders of the stock will be turning the instrument into the kind of financing vehicle the company does not need. It follows, however, that it can be a good investment for the investor because it is the investor who does the converting.

Scrip issues

These are sometimes called 'free scrip' issues, or 'capitalisation' issues. Whatever name they are going under, however, in cold theory they are a waste of time. They are a rights issue you do not have to put money up for, and they alter the underlying share price of a company, creating a lot of extra work for everyone concerned without bringing any benefit, in theory at least. After a scrip issue, earnings per share projections, assets per share projections, original purchase price, all calculations need adjusting.

The new underlying price can be calculated in just the same way as for the rights issue, only substituting a zero for the price of the rights, thus:

Share price 350p
One for three scrip issue (which means at 0p)
New theoretical price:

$$\frac{350 + 350 + 350 + 0}{4} = 262.5p$$

Companies put forward an opinion, as justification for scrip issues, which goes something like this. They believe that private investors are put off investing in what seems to be a 'heavy' or 'over-priced' share. Investors, they suggest, will be more likely to buy a share at 50p, than one at 500p. So a 500p share, given a nine for one scrip issue, would presumably be more attractive at its new theoretical price of 50p. Most private investors, in reality, know better. They know that the company is just the same as it was before, assets per share and earnings per share are unchanged in proportion to the new theoretical price, and it makes no difference to an investor whether he buys 1,000 shares at 500p, or 10,000 shares at 50p, the total investment is still £5,000.

The only benefit is a rather absurd psychological one. Many of the stock market professionals believe private investors will be influenced by the scrip issue, so they buy up all available shares. The price then rises making the share more expensive for the private investor than it was before. This sometimes provides, two or three weeks after the scrip issue has taken place, a useful selling opportunity.

Now that we have all this information, how do we create our own research capabilities? Chapter 8 details the drawing of your own charts, whilst Chapter 9 discusses the different areas of industry to look at.

8 DRAWING YOUR OWN CHARTS

Using charts

Charts of share prices have two advantages. The first is that they enable the human mind to take in a great deal of information very quickly, far more quickly than an equivalent amount of tabulated figures or text. The second is that they can reveal at a glance the actions of large investors, or large groups of investors, interested in a particular share. It is very difficult for a potential bidder to build up a 5 per cent share stake in a company without shifting the price in a way that will show up on a chart, or for a string of large institutions to move out in a way that does not send a share price into a sustained reverse. No matter what you think of the ability to extrapolate future price movements from patterns and lines drawn on a chart showing past share price movements (and many experienced fund managers will not give charts desk room), these two factors will hold good.

So charts have their uses. And an investor does not have to go to the extremes of some chartists, who never look at fundamentals or work out a p/e ratio, in order to find them helpful. But not even the most avid supporter of charts would claim that they are right every time. Follow charts and you can lose money – as indeed you can with fundamental analysis. Charts, believers feel, cut down the element of risk in investment, but cannot eliminate it completely.

Chart analysis is based on a clearly defined theory. In many investment situations, there are financially powerful investors who tend to know more than the market as a whole – in other words, markets are not perfect, and some

rich investors or institutions have access to inside information. As they move their money in or out of a share in
response to their inside knowledge, they will move the
share price, and by how much will depend on the volume of
shares traded. A careful study of share charts ought to
indicate what they are doing, even if the chartist will not
know why.

These exceptionally well-informed investors need not be
insiders in the sense that they are breaking the law by using
information which should be treated as confidential. They
could be big institutions with early access to an analyst's
research study, a group of investors living in the vicinity of
a factory aware of extra overtime working, or, if a share
price is falling, one of the company's suppliers whose
business may be rapidly falling off, or finding an extreme
reluctance to pay bills for work already done.

According to chart theory, many of the events that the
ordinary fundamental analyst will say are totally unpredict-
able, such as the sacking of the finance director for running
a damaging fraud, or the granting of valuable planning
permission for a tract of previously worthless land, will
often show up on the chart. While the Fraud Squad are
investigating the finance director, the chairman's secretary,
the auditors, half a dozen policemen and maybe as many
police secretaries will know an investigation is in progress.
The finance director's accomplices will certainly be aware of
what is happening before a formal Stock Exchange
announcement is made. And doubtless the press will also
know too. In the case of the company getting the unexpected planning windfall, a bevy of local authority civil
servants and their secretaries, plus local councillors and
possibly lawyers on both sides, will know.

The 'leak' which often would not offend conventional
standards of morality, let alone the law, may only result in
one small deal by a private individual. But how many of us
are capable of keeping a secret? A buyer of £1,000 worth of
shares may quietly hint to his stockbroker something of
what is going on, maybe to make him or herself seem
important, or maybe because the stockbroker says he was
about to sell some of those shares for another client. The

broker may ask whether his client should hang on to the shares for a bit longer. The broker then passes that snippet of information on to a pension fund that was teetering on the brink of buying that company's shares. This bit of gossip tips the balance, and an extra £100,000 of buying goes into the market. The bandwagon by then is rolling.

The drawback to this first part of chart theory is that it can lead to an awful number of false alarms. After all, not *every* bit of price sensitive information is going to find its way into the hands of someone with the will, the knowledge and the money to use it on the stock market. Also it stands to reason that whenever there is a change of plan – for example, the Police find the missing money has been sitting, forgotten, in a separate bank account, or the planning decision is overturned in committee, the man who earlier had the inside knowledge may not get to know about it either. This produces a chart pattern pointing nicely upwards, with a juicy rumour about to start spreading its way round

the stock market, all based on outdated and useless information.

Isaac Asimov wrote a series of science fiction books about the predictability of people *en masse*, and very convincing it was too. And a study of recent history, and the behaviour of mobs in other circumstances (politics, riots, etc.) suggests there may be something to this. The second part of chart theory claims that people, *en masse*, act in a predictable way; it goes on to suggest that a mass of investors will behave just as predictably as a mass of Frenchmen at the gates of the Bastille at the time of the revolution, and like as not their mood, taken as a whole and largely influenced by the powerful twin forces of greed and fear, will produce the same kind of buying and selling surges, time after time.

The basic elements of this pattern are shown in Figure 2 – totally fictitious and made up to illustrate the point. Anyone who has ever owned a share will immediately recognise the euphoria brought about by a rising share price, the swell of pride in the chest, the cock-of-the-walk feeling that passes through a conviction that you are Jack the Lad, until you believe you are invincible, the man with the Midas touch. Investors in this frame of mind frequently become so convinced of their own god-like abilities that they hang on too long to their investments. They are joined by others, motivated by fear – fear of missing out on what they believe is a certainty. Like the man who bought the Eiffel Tower, they scramble on the bandwagon, convinced that because the share price is going up, it will go up forever. Inevitably, the share price runs ahead of whatever fundamentals started the move in the first place. Sooner or later, the day approaches when there are no longer any buyers. And the price tumbles. It will not tumble too far. A healthy reaction will be stopped in its tracks as the stock's greatest fans spot a buying opportunity, and double up on their investment. But this buying soon exhausts itself, and exhaustion, to the chartist, is a near fatal condition. After it is exhausted, the glamour disappears and the sharp punters move on to another stock, leaving a share that has started to fall, and this time for real.

Figure 2 How not to invest

When a share price is falling, it can often present a mirror image of its behaviour when it was rising. It develops a momentum all of its own, as greed and fear drive investors to sell in order to protect what profit they have left. The fall, likewise, can be overdone. The investors who were at one time the stock's greatest fans will sell, often against all fundamental analysis. Some will even go short, convinced that yesterday's wonder-stock was nothing more than PR hype, or fraud. The selling will, according to theory, first meet a temporary setback, then come back with renewed strength only to be exhausted having failed to break through the steadily increasing strength of buyers exercising either inside knowledge that all is well with the company or sound fundamental analysis. The stock then goes up again. Hopefully this time to a level roughly justified by fundamentals, where it ought to have been all along.

So you think our made-up chart is extreme? Have a look at the charts of Polly Peck, of London & Liverpool, of Bambers Stores and of Resource Technology. Do some of the features look familiar? With your hand, cover up the righthand side of any of these charts. Would you not say that the upward movement sitting in splendid isolation on the left-hand side bears an uncanny resemblance to the performance of some glamour stocks you have seen recently?

There is a third justification for charting, which falls some way short of being a rule, but forms the basis for some important elements of technical analysis. When investing, there is a basic human tendency to look at a share in terms of its original purchase price. So an investor, particularly a private investor, who buys a share and sees it go down, will tend to hang on to it until the price rises enough for him to get his money back.

The price at which a purchase is made is important for institutions, too. Frequently a fund manager will fix a correct buying price in his or her mind, and patiently soak up stock at this price as it becomes available, over a time

Figure 3   Polly Peck International from 2/1/81 to 2/6/86 weekly
High 334.28 28/1/83; low 13.96 2/1/81; last 191.00

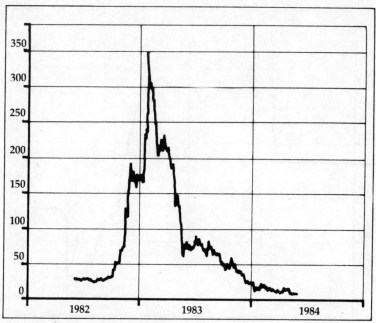

Figure 4   London and Liverpool from 2/6/82 to 1/6/84 daily
High 350.00 31/1/83; low 8.00 14/5/84; last 8.00

Figure 5   Bambers Stores from 2/1/79 to 31/12/82 weekly
Note: High 106.67 5/6/79; low 14.00 28/12/82; last 14.00

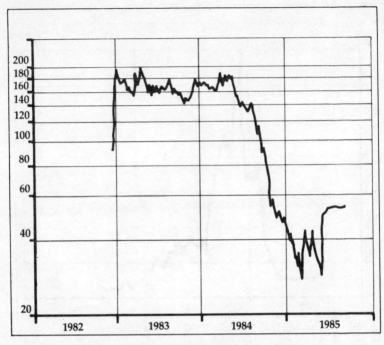

Figure 6   Resource Technology from 1/1/82 to 30/8/85 weekly
High 197.00 15/4/83; low 27.00 8/3/85; last 53.00

scale of a few weeks or months. This holds a price at a
certain level until either all the sellers have been taken out,
or until the fund manager has accumulated all the stock he
or she wants. The same thing can happen with selling.

So there are two different sets of investors operating with
reference to a set price level, but for different reasons.
Because of this, a share price can become stuck in a groove
for quite a while trading 'sideways'. It is also possible to see
a battle taking place in the market between buyers and
sellers, which will climax as one exhausts the other and
moves the share price hard in a particular direction.
Another effect of this groove, price-sticking pattern, is that
the one share groove pattern on the way down will tend to
show roughly the same on its way up again – and vice
versa.

Now we have explained the logic (or, if you are still a
non-believer, the apparent logic) behind some stock market

behaviour, we can have a look at some of the more important patterns they build up in share price movements; the
first will be the 'Double top'.

Identifying and analysing different chart patterns

Double top

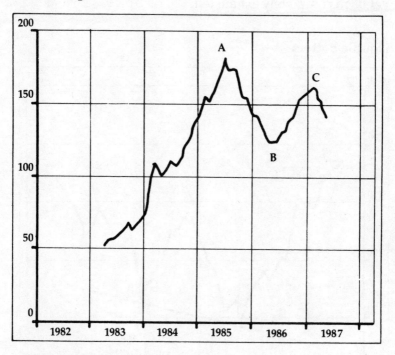

Figure 7   Double top
Note: Second top C is lower than first A.

This chart shows a share roaring up through an excess of
enthusiasm. It peaks at (A) as the buying temporarily dries
up and is overwhelmed by selling pressure. Lower down,
B, the buyers reassert themselves and once more gain the
upper hand. At C, however, exhaustion sets in. The sellers
are present in overwhelming strength, the buyers are unable to push through this resistance. Exhausted, the price
falls back – there is no strength left to support it. The sellers

141

rush through, and the previous buyers then turn sellers to either protect their position with what profits are left, or to cut their losses. By then, the stock is heading downhill fast.

Note that the second top does not quite reach the peak established by the first one. It is the buyers that have become exhausted rather than the sellers. If the second top is higher than the first, a new high has been established and there is still some 'run' left in this rise as the buying has not yet been completely exhausted.

Double bottom

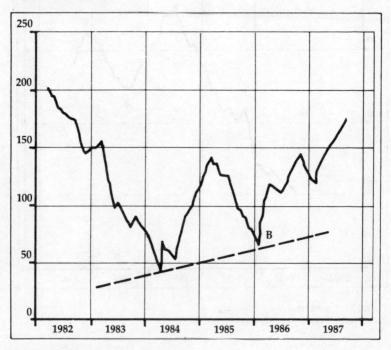

Figure 8   Double bottom
Note: Second bottom B higher than first.

This picture is essentially a mirror image of the 'double top'. Note once again, there is a temporary retreat, a renewed advance, then exhaustion. Again, the second advance makes rather less progress than the first one. If the second low is lower than the first, then the buyers, not the sellers, have been beaten – and that to technical analysts is bad news.

Head and shoulders

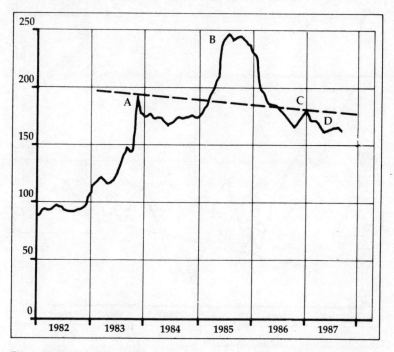

Figure 9   Head and shoulders
Note: Second shoulder lower than first. Pattern established at D, time to sell.

This picture is again a classic indication of a top. At A the buying runs into resistance, and falls back under the weight of selling before heading back up as if it is going for a 'double top'. Only this time it is not a double top. The buyers win and the price pushes through to new high ground at B before, weakened, it pauses for breath and then sinks down once more.

After this second fall, buying reasserts itself, but by then selling pressure is building up, and buying is sadly going out of fashion. This rally stops at about the level of the first one at C, ideal from the point of view of the technical analyst, a little short of A and certainly well short of B. The buyers have then had it. All the smart money is taking profits, and the shares head down once more.

Reverse head and shoulders

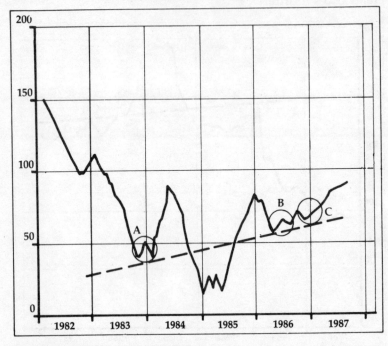

Figure 10   Reverse head and shoulders
Note: Second shoulder higher than the first. The pattern has been established at
C, time to buy.

The mirror image of the 'head and shoulders', marking the bottom of the market. Note, again, the second trough is stronger than the first, and the third one is either about the level of the first, or the weakest of the lot.

Resistance

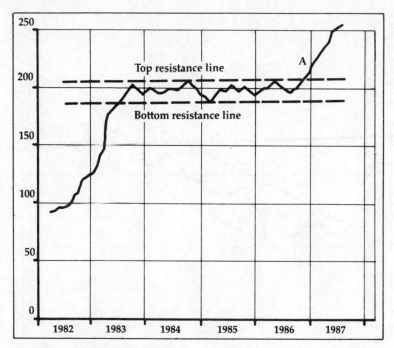

Figure 11   Resistance line
Note: Price movement shows trading is slow with little or no alteration.
    Follow resistance line until price break occurs; then buy A.

This picture shows, according to chart theory, a large seller unloading stock at a fixed price whenever a buyer appears. Either he wins, as in this case, sells all his shares and the price marches forward again, or he loses (not shown) and the price edges down again.

The trendline

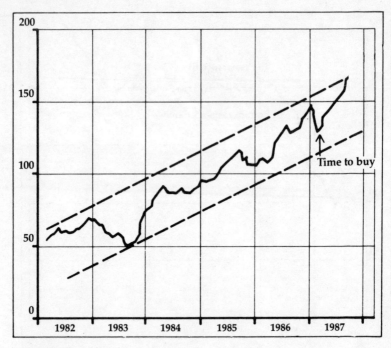

Figure 12   Trend line.

This shows an institution, or a series of institutions, determined in its purchase of shares. They will make one purchase, then wait for more shares to become available at that price. As there are not enough sellers, so the institution raises its sights, and pays a few pence more for the next lump. Obviously, if the institution is a seller, the process works in reverse.

'The trendline' is not to be confused with the excess of enthusiasm that precedes a 'double top'. It is a steady, reliable, established pattern that, according to the chartists, can give investors a certain amount of confidence in the trend continuing.

The flag

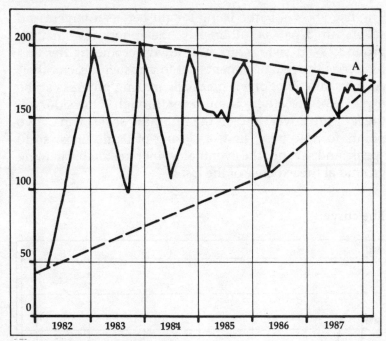

Figure 13   Upward pointing flag
Note: The buyer is ahead, A, time to buy.

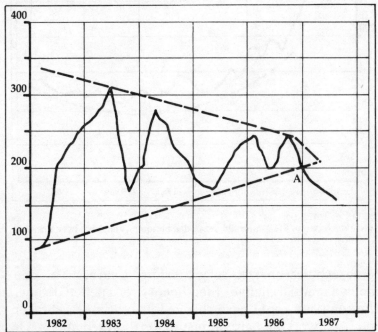

Figure 14   Downward pointing flag
Note: The seller is ahead, A, time to sell.

The flag show a battle being fought between buyers and sellers in what is otherwise, metaphorically, neutral ground. Wild swings up and down become tighter and tighter as the two opponents get to grips with each other. At the same time, one is gradually making progress at the expense of the other. Then, breakthrough. One side, (on the left, the buyer, and on the right, the seller) wins. Two points to note here; first, a closing of battle lines, so to speak, and second, the eventual winner inexorably gaining ground at the expense of the loser.

The curve

Figure 15 The curve
Note: Watch out for the comfortable, rounded bottom; when A has been reached, buy.

Some technical analysts set great store by curves. This one shows a gradual change of sentiment over a period of time. The company could have changed its official stockbroker and been working hard on institutional presentations. Or the monthly production figures published by the Department of Trade for its industry may be starting to turn around. Either way, it is devoid of the drama of the earlier patterns and, its enthusiasts would say, becomes all the more reliable because of it.

This leads us on to more complex technical indicators.

Technical analysis

Following trendlines pointing forever upwards is all very well, but any investor who took that as the only measure of when to be in and out of a stock would, of course, be buying at the top of every bull market, and selling at the bottom of every bear market. What happens when a top point or a bottom level is reached, but there is no clear 'double top' or 'double bottom', or 'head and shoulders', to warn that an important turning point has been attained? The technical analysts have several important but more sophisticated weapons in their armoury for helping to spot them.

The first pointer that they use is the 'moving average'. This can be the average share price for the previous 5, 10, 25, 50 (you choose the number) days' trading. With each additional day's trading that takes place, the value of the average changes, hence its name. If a share price backtracks to below its 'moving average' from above it (Figure 16), this can (but not always) indicate a change in sentiment. It is very much like dropping through a trend or support line as far as a technical analyst is concerned. Obviously, the shorter the time period chosen for the moving average, the more frequently it is likely to be crossed, and the more short term the change in sentiment can be viewed.

Do not bother to calculate your own moving averages. There are several excellent programs for popular home computers that can do this, and the addresses of some are given at the back of this book. If you do not have your own home computer, or do not have the past data on the particular stock that you are analysing, your stockbroker will be able to produce one for you from his Datastream machine. A more sophisticated use of moving averages is the 'golden cross'.

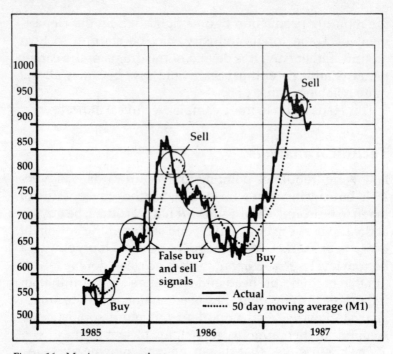

Figure 16   Moving average chart
ICI from 30/5/85 to 30/5/87; daily chart
High 1000.00 7/3/87; low 534.00 13/7/85; last 907.00

Technical analysts have noticed that the combination of two different moving averages can be very useful. And in particular, what became apparent was when one time base for a moving average is four times the size of another, major changes in sentiment often occur when the two averages cross. There are two usual moving average pairs taken for the golden cross, 25 and 100 day, and 50 and 200 day.

A true golden cross occurs when both moving averages are rising. If both are falling, this is called a 'Dead Cross' and is regarded by the professionals as bad news. These crosses are interesting and can be misleading; it is important to bear in mind that using the longer dated averages, up to a third of the fall could have taken place before the signal is given.

Other measurements are used to keep a check on the extremes of passion that often accompany both long and short-term peaks and troughs. The stock market hardly ever moves up or down more than 10 per cent without a correction, or in the same direction for more than eight consecutive trading days. At the same time, technical analysts look out for a firmness, a continuity of purpose, in the movement of a share price or a stock market index. For the stock market as a whole, there are several ways of doing this.

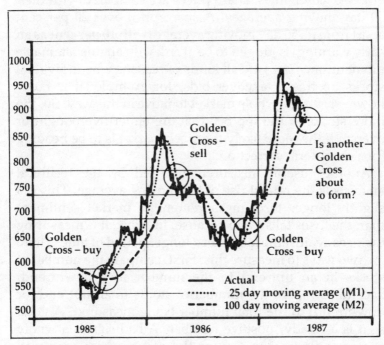

Figure 17 Golden cross chart
ICI from 30/5/85 to 30/5/87 daily

The first form of measurement is through the 'sentiment indicator'. This measures the number of days during the previous ten in which the stock market has risen or fallen. Technical analysts believe that an extreme measurement, either over 75 per cent or under 25 per cent, is usually unsustainable.

The second form of measurement is the 'advance/decline' ratio. Newspapers print the number of shares rising each day and the total of those falling, so fortunately this sum is already calculated for the private investor. The ratio itself is the number of stocks that have risen against the number that have fallen. A comfortable average is between 30 per cent and 120 per cent. Anything outside these ranges could signal the start of a dramatic change in sentiment, particularly if it is a reversal of direction.

The 'overbought/oversold' radio is a measure of when the market is moving up, or down, unsustainably fast. The 'top 500' companies' share prices are compared with their 50 day moving averages. A share price over 20 per cent apart from its 50 day moving average (with 10 per cent as an early warning) is judged to be at risk with an unsustainable momentum. There are all kinds of reasons why individual stocks do this – takeover bids, for example. It is rarer, however, for the whole market to move in this way. So, the more stocks in the top 500 that are either overbought or oversold, the more likely the stock market is to be heading for a short-term correction.

Another useful measurement used by the technical analysts is the rate of rise of the moving average. This is a slightly longer term measurement of market sentiment than the 'rises/falls' ratio because, in effect, it is measuring the rises against the falls over a longer period of time. There are two ways to measure this. First, compare the number of stocks in an uptrend to the number in a downtrend. Second, compare the number of stocks in an uptrend (or downtrend) to the total number being measured. A good sign is a steady, positive number. A bad sign is a wildly excessive figure one way or the other, which may well prove unsustainable.

Ways of drawing charts

There are several ways of drawing charts. Use one and not another, and it is possible to miss what could be an important signal. It is also possible for charts drawn in different ways to contradict each other. After all, if making money on the stock market was simple, if there was any foolproof system, everybody would be a millionaire.

Here are the main ways of drawing charts, with some examples.

Straightforward line chart

Figure 18   Straightforward line chart ICI from 18/5/84 to 19/5/86; daily chart
Note: High 1000.00 7/3/86; low 534.00 13/7/84; last 884.00

The straightforward line chart is the kind of chart we have been using throughout this chapter so far. Note that on the horizontal, or 'x' axis, we are plotting time; and on the upright or 'y' axis, we are plotting price. Both are transposed on a straightforward basis.

Relative price index

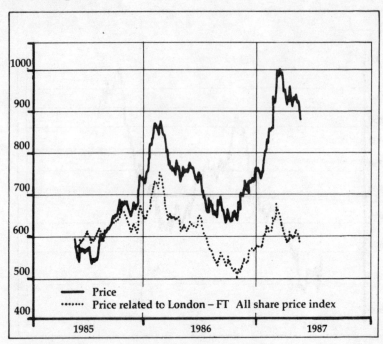

Figure 19   Relative Price Index ICI from 18/5/85 to 19/5/87; daily chart
Note: High 1000.00 7/3/87; low 534.00 13/7/85; last 884.00

Against the very same chart, Figure 15, we have added the share price divided by the All-Share Index. Do not work this out for yourself, let the computer do it. It stands to reason that in a roaring bull market few, if any, stocks are going to trace a bearish pattern – most will be pointing up to the sky. If a share which has been previously strong against the market gradually turns down to look weak against it, then this fact is important to know, and it might not catch your eye immediately. A 'relative price' chart will show this up straight away – and you do not have to be a great believer in technical analysis to see the advantages of that. Indeed, some technical analysts prefer to trace all their chart patterns on these charts.

Semi-log charts

Figure 20   Semi-log chart ICI from 18/5/84 to 19/5/86; daily chart
Note: High 1000.00 7/3/86; low 534.00 13/7/84; last 884.00

With this chart, the 'y' axis, or 'price' axis, is compressed the higher the share rises. This method ensures that a price will have the same movement up for each percentage gain, rather than for the gain in price terms. Thus, to make a 1cm move upwards on the chart, a price might have to move from 20p to 30p. To make the next 1cm move upwards, the price would have to jump not from 30p to 40p, but from 30p to 45p, a move of 50 per cent just like the move from 20p to 30p.

The principle behind this method is to avoid distortions created by large price movements. If that 20p share quintuples to 100p, the next 10p move, from 100p to 110p, is obviously going to be far less significant than the initial rise from 20p to 30p and, arguably, deserves far less space on the chart.

This has little impact on 'double tops' and 'head and

155

shoulder' patterns but does have a serious effect on 'trend-lines'. Visually, compared to a normal linear chart, it compresses the top of a chart, and widens the bottom of it.

Point and figure charts

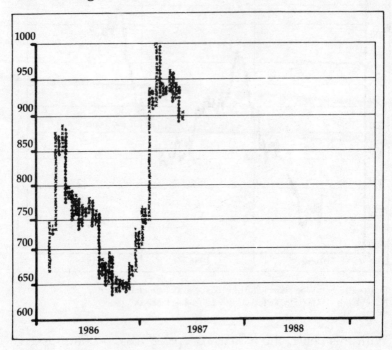

Figure 21   Point and figure

This type of chart has been left until last because it is the strangest looking thing in the chartist's library, giving the appearance to the newcomer of being mumbo-jumbo, and has probably done more to put people off technical analysis than any other factor.

With a 'point and figure' chart there is only a 'y' axis. The 'x' axis ceases to count. Time is of no importance in a 'point and figure' chart. If nothing interesting happens to a share price, then no marks are made on the chart. The logic behind this is as follows. The chart follower is looking out for certain important developments, such as one of the patterns that can be drawn to show emergence of a domi-

nant seller or buyer, etc. For long periods of time a share price can be moving up a bit, down a bit, doing nothing of the least significance to anybody, just generally trading 'sideways'. Why then bother charting the irrelevant bits? They will only involve you in a lot of unnecessary work, at best lead you off on a wild goose chase hunting after a pattern that does not exist or, worse still, blinding you with so much detail that you miss a really important pattern building up.

The irrelevant bits are cut out by only making a mark on the chart when the share moves a certain amount in either direction, say, 5p. So, a share that spends six months edging around between 100p and 104p will have no mark on the chart, in spite of the enormous amount of time that has passed. Also, movements in the same direction are piled on top, or underneath, of one another. The chart only moves into a new column of the 'x' axis when there is a change of direction.

In order to find out the time at which a particular price was reached, the months and years are sometimes marked in the graph square instead of the normal 'x' or 'o'. The 'x' is by convention used when a price is moving upwards, the 'o' when it is moving downwards. This is simply a piece of embroidery, not necessary for accurate 'point and figure' charting, because it is quite obvious in which direction a price is moving without this.

More than any other section of investment, technical analysis has a tendency to descend rapidly into obscure elitist jargon. But that should not blind any investor to the underlying principles of what the technical analyst is trying to do. Absorbing large volumes of information quickly, sweeping away emotional prejudice, both favourable and unfavourable, looking for tell-tale signs of inside activity, and attempting to second guess the reactions of the common herd on the stock market are the preoccupations of the chartist.

No matter what you think of the methods, you have to admire the aims and select whichever method is best suited to your requirements. And if technical analysis does not work all the time, well, does anything?

9 EVERY SECTOR TELLS A DIFFERENT STORY

So far, we have covered the field of investment analysis as if all industries are the same. They are not. Each sector has its own peculiarities, and anyone who tries to analyse a sector without knowing precisely what to look for is under a great handicap. Here are a few notes, by no means exhaustive, on what matters for some of the more important industries. To create your own analysis on your chosen industry, in addition to taking the daily papers which have financial pages, such as *The Daily Telegraph* and *Financial Times*, you should also subscribe to the industry's own journals, newspaper or magazine, in order to pick up any news otherwise missed by the national papers. If you are not sure of the different media names involved, go to your local library and look through a copy of BRAD (British Rate and Data).

Agencies

For advertising and marketing companies, balance sheets are more or less irrelevant. None of these companies have any significant liabilities and so are most unlikely to go bankrupt. Their businesses generate cash, the companies do not have capital investment programmes of any significance, and have straightforward profit and loss accounts with a negligible depreciation element.

Shares move up and down on the gain and loss of large accounts, although on average 90 per cent of all advertising business will stay with the same agency for at least five years. They also move up and down when key personnel move from one agency to another – and this is a fairly common occurrence as advertising people are by nature volatile. These movements are splashed every Thursday morning in the industry's weekly paper, *Campaign*, which is essential reading for anybody thinking of investing in this sector.

The advertising and marketing industry has grown every year for the last ten years at a faster rate than the gross national product, although this is no guarantee, of course, that the pattern will continue forever. Some of the companies in the industry have produced some spectacularly good growth rates – when there is no plant and equipment to buy and run, profits can spiral rapidly. Also the management in this sector comes over very well at institutional presentations run by the big brokers. The three factors together combine to produce above average p/e ratios as a whole, and well above average for the more fashionable companies in the sector. These companies are then able to use their high ratings to buy private companies, giving an automatic boost to earnings per share (see Chapter 6).

The trick for successful investment in this sector is to spot which share will become the next glamour company; read *Campaign* avidly for a hint of anything that might turn sentiment against your chosen favourite.

Estate agencies and employment agencies share the ability to produce huge increases in profits with little apparent effort. Estate agents are busy when the housing market is active, and suffer when house prices start to fall. Employment agencies suffer in an industrial recession when unemployment starts to rise.

Banks

Banks make their living by borrowing money from customers and lending it to others at a higher rate. The difference between these two sets of transactions, after deducting running costs and bad debts, is their profit. As a third of the money they lend out comes to them totally free of charge (via current account deposits, which do not pay interest) the higher interest rates are, the more profit they make. However, the higher bad debts are, the lower the profit they make. Analysing bank shares frequently comes down to making a judgement on which way interest rates are going to go, and judging how many bad debts a particular bank has accumulated (bank accounts are far from forthcoming on this matter). Two recent examples of British banks which have had to deal with large overseas debts were the Midland Bank and Lloyds Bank. At the worst, bad debts can bring down a bank, but this usually only happens indirectly when depositors get wind of possible bad debt problems and pull their money out, creating a cash crisis as happened in the 1929 recession. So getting an idea of the profile of the bank's loan portfolio in which you are interested, and comparing it to the loan profile of other banks, is important.

Bank balance sheets look totally different to ordinary manufacturing company balance sheets. The vast flood of money coming in from depositors and going out to borrowers is accomplished on a relatively narrow capital base. The capital base (shareholders' funds plus perpetual loan stocks) is expressed as a percentage of total money outstanding and is known as the 'capital ratio'. Generally, with British banks it is between 4 per cent and 8 per cent. Therefore a write-down of 4 per cent of the loan portfolio as a bad debt could knock the bank from the safest end of the range to the least safe. Which is why it is important to be aware of the potential bad debt situation on a *worldwide* scale.

Generally speaking, British high street banks have been very successful in expanding their loan books in recent years. An expanding loan book reduces the capital ratio. In order to fund this expansion, banks keep coming to the stock market for more equity capital, by way of rights issues. These are usually bad for their share prices, and explain why bank shares are on such low p/e ratios given their historic growth records. Any company with a capital ratio at the lower end of the range might be looking for an excuse to spring a rights issue on its unsuspecting shareholders. That excuse usually comes shortly after a rise in the share price – so be warned.

Merchant banks generally are a disappearing breed as the

City moves towards massive financial conglomerates. Merchant banks are even less forthcoming than retail banks because they only declare their profits after unquantified 'transfers to or from reserves' – which themselves are not declared in the balance sheet. Yes, you have guessed it, this means they can make their profits come out to almost any figure they want. So there is little point trying to analyse a situation when the odds are as heavily stacked against you as this.

Breweries

Is there a more enjoyable sector to analyse than this! Basically, all brewery company balance sheets are quite sound, with limited gearing and backed by a mass of valuable (and often undervalued) property. The report and accounts are important as they indicate where a brewery company is earning its profits – how much from beer, how much from hotels, how much from any of a string of associated interests – and there are many. The brewery group that is first and heaviest on to a particular bandwagon in this industry gains at the expense of the others. If there is a trend towards wine bars or cocktail lounges, discotheques or slot machines, an examination of the accounts of the main brewing companies (and the smaller regional brewers) ought to give some indication of which one is being most adept at riding the trend.

The most serious research work, however, needs to be done in the pubs themselves – and one could say the most enjoyable! Pub tenants and managers are a mine of information on which kind of drink is gaining market share at the expense of others, whether business is going up or going down, which brewery draymen are making noises about going on strike, etc. A good wide sample is important to avoid distortions.

Every so often a regional brewer gets taken over at a vastly higher price than the shares have been trading at. This is justified as the property assets are usually considerably undervalued in brewery accounts, also the value of the licences themselves is considerable. Buying shares in regional brewers on takeover hopes is, however, a question of gambling with rather long odds. Takeovers are few and far between.

Contracting

Contracting companies, whether building roads, dams, or chemical plants, are handling large lumps of work over a long period of time. Even for the largest companies, one contract may account for up to 50 per cent of its turnover in any one year, and contracts can take three or four years to complete.

When individual contracts are so large, and spread over such a long period of time, the way that profits are spread out over the contract become crucial. Most construction companies take some profits every year, throughout the course of a contract, with a slightly larger than usual sum at the end. Disputes over work done arise with monotonous regularity, and every so often a construction company goes bankrupt because a customer somewhere in the world claims that a dam has been built behind schedule, the surface of a motorway is cracking prematurely or a chemical plant is working below its design specification.

The big jump in profits can come at the end of a contract. But remember that unless the contractor has more work to replace it, the following year will be poor. Also if the work load is reducing, the balance sheet is likely to be adversely affected as many contracting companies make a very nice living out of advance payments from their customers (showing up clearly in the accounts) which they are tardy about passing on to their subcontractors.

Currency movements are a problem for contractors, many of them have a large proportion of their workload overseas. It is important to ascertain how much of the workload is overseas, and equally as important, in which countries.

Engineering

The largest customer for the engineering sector is the motor industry. Watch the twice monthly figures for UK car sales (indications given about the 20th of each month, with formal figures just after the end of the month) and you will have a very good idea about the state of health of the engineering industry.

Generally speaking, inflation is bad for engineers because they have proved unwilling to price their products up to the level that allows them to replace plant and equipment at higher prices in terms of future money. An engineering company with a high gearing ratio could be in bad trouble, unable to replace worn, obsolete machine tools with modern equipment, and gradually sliding downhill in terms of the products it is making as a result. Make sure that capital spending at least equals the depreciation figure. Capital spending lower than depreciation can be a sign that an engineering company is falling into this particular trap.

Watch property values, also. Many engineering companies are operating from premises that are included in the accounts at outdated valuations. In the North of England that may not matter much, but in the South, or near the centre of big towns, that can be a goldmine if the property can be converted to another use. The only way to find out is to go and take a look at the factories.

Insurance

The important point to note in this industry is that insurance broking and insurance underwriting are two totally separate businesses, and life insurance is yet another. Identifying which company is in which particular area ought to be straightforward, particularly as broking and underwriting are supposed, by law, to be kept separate. In practice, however, the number of pure companies are few and far between. Most insurance underwriting companies have a mix of life assurance and general insurance. Most brokers make part of their profits from either managing Lloyd's syndicates (a practice soon to end) in return for a performance-based fee or owning insurance company subsidiaries.

It is important to identify just where the profits of your target company are coming from. Generally speaking, insurance broking is the highest quality type of profit. This has been growing very rapidly as both the developed countries and the Third World become more insurance conscious, and a broker will make money whether the underwriting of the risks concerned is profitable or not (although it will make more profit when rates are high because then its percentage commission will go up proportionately). The insurance brokerage that makes much of its profit in the UK is a rare animal because the insurance industry is extraordinarily international. So check your target company to see what portion of its earnings are derived from overseas sources, and again from which countries.

Another important aspect to look at is whether there are any large clients, or particular industries, which make up a significant proportion of sales or profits? The loss of a major client or the departure of an important executive can have a serious impact on profits. A contact in the industry is the best way of checking on this. The newsletter that handles this type of price-sensitive information, *Re Report*, is too expensive for the average private investor, and is not stocked by most public libraries.

Most important of all for the broker, how much of the profit is derived from underwriting? The higher the proportion, the lower the rating the broker deserves.

Profits in the conventional (as distinct from the unit-linked) life insurance industry are limited by law. The vast bulk of the profits made on the investments the life company controls must go to the policyholders, and the life company shareholders benefit pro rata. Profits are not taken as shares are sold, however. The portfolio as a whole is valued, actuaries are employed to make allowance for investment matters, such as likely future interest rate and inflation trends, and compare the value of the investments with the promises made to policyholders on future policy values, and as a result a 'bonus' is declared for policyholders. The life company's profits rise (they hardly ever fall) in line with the bonus.

In general insurance, watch for two key ratios: outstanding claims against shareholders' funds and insurance reserves, and the premiums underwritten against shareholders' funds and insurance reserves. The higher the ratios, the thinner the ice the insurance underwriter *may* be skating upon. The word *may* is used because there are so many different kinds of insurance company. One may specialise in car accident damage insurance and will know what claims it has to pay out relatively quickly after the end of a financial year, also whether each claim will be for a relatively small sum of money or not. A company specialising in product liability insurance in the United States, or the very top slice of a heavily layered re-insurance policy, may have to wait years before it knows whether it has a claim to pay at all, let alone how large the claim is going to be. Insurance companies are currently fighting about pollution scandals and industrial injury claims that have their roots as far back as the 1950s – not only are the claims not yet settled, but the companies concerned did not know until a year or two ago whether there was a potential claim at all!

It is important in this respect to watch the progress of the so-called IBNR reserve – short for claims 'incurred but not reported'. It is also vitally important to ascertain precisely which classes of insurance business are being underwritten. The insurance trade press, and the chairman's statements of rival companies both in Britain and overseas, make very clear which particular classes of business, and in which countries, are giving cause for concern at any particular moment in time. No wonder general insurance underwriting tends to be given such a poor rating by the stock market.

Minerals

This heading applies to oil, gold, nickel, platinum, tin, or basically whatever comes out from under the ground, whether it is solid or liquid.

The three main areas of business are exploration, production, and marketing, and the first thing to do with any mineral company is to separate out each of these three interests. If the company is exclusively in one area, but not in others, so much the better – but only from the point of view of simplicity of analysis. Companies with an interest in only one of these three areas tend to have short lives, albeit exciting ones.

Exploration

The quickest way of making and losing millions is in mineral exploration. In the 1880s, Cecil Rhodes in the Kimberley diamond mines, and Barney Banato, in the Rand goldfields, became the two richest men in the world, within 10 years, by successful mineral exploration. (They kept their wealth and expanded on it, by successful production and marketing, as did John D. Rockefeller at Standard Oil 20 years later, but that is another story.) In assessing exploration stocks, it is important to be aware not just of the likelihood of a strike, but also the cost of extracting the mineral from the ground, transporting it to a suitable point of collection and refining it from ore (or crude oil or unclean gas) into pure metal (or petrol, etc.).

Headlines made at the time of original mineral strikes have turned out to be barely commercial, or not even worth exploiting at all. When trading in exploration shares (the word investment hardly applies to these volatile shares: speculation in this industry is not recommended for first-time investors, only those very strong-hearted bullish investors), it is as well to remember the old maxim, 'buy on the rumour, sell on the strike'. The best time to buy an exploration share is usually when the drilling team first goes in. Remember Poseidon shares. They went from 25p to £106 in six months and then collapsed back to 25p – the company that had struck the famous nickel deposit could not raise the finance to transport and refine its ore!

Find out how many shares there are in issue. With exploration companies, this can be difficult; and further difficulty can develop if you hold stock in overseas exploration businesses as these companies have an unfortunate

167

habit of issuing new shares without telling small shareholders. Multiply the share price by the number of shares yet to be issued and you arrive at the total value for the company. Compare this figure with the market capitalisation of other producing companies already well established in the same industry. Remember that an exploration company, given a deposit of equal size to one held by a production company, is in theory worth *far less*. The production company already has its production facilities, refining and transport arrangements in place. The exploration company does not, it has yet to fund them. An oil exploration company, whose share price rises to an inflated value invariably falls back to reality again very quickly. Do not be one of those investors caught out.

Other points worth remembering are that no exploration prospect can have its worth assessed on just one borehole. The company might have put down its hole in the most favourable spot; for oil companies, a flow test through a narrow choke over a very short time span is meaningless (only a long flow through a large choke can give even a rough idea of the amount of oil present). Short tests through narrow chokes are sometimes released by exploration companies in order to jack up their share prices to raise funds for further development.

For most exploration companies, but for oil in particular, only a small proportion of the reserves that are found will be developed. For mineral companies there will be pockets of ore that are too low grade to be worth processing. For oil, only 30 per cent to 40 per cent of most oil finds can actually be extracted from the ground, even with so-called secondary recovery methods such as water injection. So when a mineral strike is described as being 'x' tons or 'y' million barrels of oil or tonnes of ore, make sure it is a recoverable and not a gross figure that is being quoted.

Production

Unless a production company is discovering new mineral finds, it is a wasting asset as all mines and oil wells run out sooner or later. Therefore the production element of any company must be treated as a wasting asset. To value it, do present value or discounted cash flow calculations based upon the future income flow. Or more important, the dividend flow. When any company, no matter what the industry, sits on retained earnings there is no guarantee the shareholder will ever see any of that money.

Marketing

Marketing companies do well in times of glut, when, on the other hand, production companies are at a great disadvantage. But the reverse happens in times of shortage, the production companies can cut off any independent marketing company that does not have its own internal company supplies. When this happens, marketing companies frequently go bust. Some oil giants, BP for example, have traditionally been well endowed with production, and weak on marketing, while others, such as Gulf, have their strengths and weaknesses the other way round.

Frequently, production and marketing are difficult to disentangle. What proportion does De Beers have? Is it a production company because it controls over 80 per cent of the world's diamond mines? Or is it a marketing company because of its control of sales and its ability to make people believe that a diamond in an engagement ring is a priority?

Retailing

There are two important cost areas for retailers, and likewise for the analyst. The first is inventory, and the second is size of the selling area.

Inventory can be dangerous because stock which is out of date in all probability will not be worth as much as the sum included in the balance sheet. To the retailer, just as important, out-of-date stock will not sell well, so sales suffer. So, watch the stock figure (see Chapter 6). But when making comparisons, remember a supermarket chain is going to be turning over its stock very much more rapidly than a men's outfitter, and a chain of antique shops might conceivably benefit from holding on to its inventory for a long time.

The second point is sales or display area. People expect to shop in stores of a certain size. A supermarket with a small sales area will not do the business of a supermarket with a large one as customers will not be able to find the choice of goods they have become used to. From the cost point of view, a retailer with space in the high street is going to find this rather more expensive to service than a retailer with out-of-town premises. Fans of Marks & Spencer will talk convincingly of 'sales per square foot' as being an important measure, perhaps the only important measure. But look instead at 'profits per square foot'. There is no point in selling things if you cannot make a profit on them. Remember a company at the top of the sales per square foot league might be riding for a fall, and the company with low profit per square foot may be capable of squeezing more profit out of its sales. The latter may present the best investment potential – provided, of course, the management is able to implement the improvement.

Textiles

Now this is where the inventory figure is supremely important. No matter how beguiling the stories of new contracts, ultra-modern machinery, or anti-dumping bans on overseas competition, remember a company caught with a warehouse full of ankle-length skirts at a time when jeans are coming into fashion is a liability in the portfolio. The longer the stock turn figure, the more likely it is to be caught out by a change in fashion. Ears to the ground and eyes to the fashion pages for this industry.

10 YOUR PORTFOLIO STRATEGY

Throughout the book, we have been working towards this final aim – establishing a portfolio. But before you buy a single share, it is important to have an overall strategy for the investments. You must decide what you want from your portfolio, and establish certain criteria that every share you choose *must* fulfill. If you do not, then you will be swept into a state of financial chaos. Your stockbroker, your friends, the newspapers and magazines will constantly be throwing ideas at you, and before you know where you are, you will be stuck with a horrendous mish-mash of shares none of which make sense either in terms of what you want from your money or from life in general.

Here are ten prime questions that you must ask yourself before you go any further.

1 Do you want an income from your shares? If so, how much?
2 How much capital growth are you prepared to sacrifice to get this income?
3 How much risk are you prepared to accept? (In other words, how much are you prepared to lose before you cut your losses?)
4 How many shares do you want in your portfolio?
5 What kind of currency spread do you want?
6 How varied do you want your portfolio to be?
7 What is the industry split in the portfolio to be?
8 How often do you expect to change the shares in the portfolio?
9 What attitude will you take if a share in the portfolio gets a takeover bid, and should the portfolio have a number of shares in it that are likely to attract a takeover bid?

10 What is your attitude going to be if a company has a
     rights issue, asking for more money?

Points to consider when making up your portfolio

Income

The yield (or profit) on the average share is between 3 per
cent and 4 per cent, just enough to keep pace with inflation
(before tax, not after it), but trivial compared to the income
from fixed interest investments. It is possible, however, to
find perfectly good shares that yield rather more. In theory,
going for high yield shares ought to result in a lower capital
gain because any share with a high yield ought to have
substandard growth prospects. In practice, however, portfolios constructed of good quality high yielding shares
have, quite often, performed well above average. If income
is irrelevant, then do not let yield be an influence. If income
matters, there are plenty of good shares to choose from and
there is no need to look at any share that yields less than 150
per cent of the market average.

Risk

All shares are risky but some are more risky than others. To
analyse risk, pull out a share price graph covering the last
five years, and see how much the share price has moved in
the past, and why. If a share's price history is steady, the
greater the likelihood of avoiding nasty surprises (and
pleasant ones) in the future. This is often referred to as the
risk/reward ratio – the higher the risk, the greater the
reward.

Investors who are prepared to accept a high level of risk
should *not* automatically reverse that thinking, however.
Accepting a higher level of risk does not always result in
higher reward. Indeed, studies have shown that obviously
high risk/high reward shares tend to be overpriced because
of the large number of speculators anxious to get rich quick
at almost any cost.

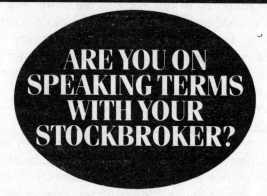

Another important element to watch: the company should be involved in relatively stable industries. A company in the food industry is likely to be more reliable than one drilling for oil or building microcomputers. Some industries, while being relatively stable as a whole, can produce individual crises of overwhelming proportions as far as individual companies are concerned. International contracting is notorious for producing upsets, such as foreign countries refusing to honour contracts, or for work costing very much more to complete than previously expected or forecast because of poor local financial controls or, for that matter, a wealth of other reasons. Any company where the size of the average contract, or average debt, is large in relation to the share capital must contain an element of risk.

Another useful way of keeping down risk is to make sure the companies chosen have spare cash in the bank, or little or no debt. The more a company borrows, the more likely an unforeseen trading mistake or unexpected setback can cause serious problems.

Number of shares

Technical studies have shown that it is possible to get a very good spread in a portfolio having as few as seven companies' shares in it. Have fewer than seven shares, and you increase the risk of losing money by an unexpected disaster, or by poor share selection, with every share you leave out. That is not to say, of course, that it is wrong to own fewer than seven different shares at any one time, particularly for a small investor. It is simply that there is a much larger chance of the performance of the portfolio not mirroring the performance of the popular share indices.

To give a sensible spread of risk, however, those seven shares have to be very carefully chosen. Let us choose an obvious example. A portfolio consisting of seven South African gold mine shares is extremely risky because any drop in the gold price, or political problems in South Africa, could hit all seven shares in the portfolio badly. That is an extreme and absurdly simple example. Other less obvious

ones do have an unfortunate tendency to creep up un-
noticed in a portfolio chosen in an ill-considered or hap-
hazard way. One company in the portfolio may make
widgets, another may sell widgets, and still a third may
supply raw materials to the company making them. A
fourth share might be an insurance broker, with its largest
client the widget manufacturer. Then the unexpected happens, widgets go out of fashion (or get banned – substitute
tobacco for widgets, for instance) and the portfolio is in
deep trouble. It is one thing to set out deliberately to
structure a portfolio to take advantage of a boom expected
shortly in the widget industry, but it is quite another to
walk into such a situation blindfold!

Currency exposure, vulnerability to recession, and a
number of other factors could be common between the
shares you have chosen. Examine your proposed portfolio
carefully from all angles, preferably *before* buying the shares
rather than afterwards!

What is the maximum number of shares a portfolio
should have? Unless you are super-rich, make 15 different
shares the absolute maximum. Even at this level it is
enormously difficult to keep track of the different industries
being followed, the profit announcements and balance
sheets being issued, and the dividends due. If you feel 15
shares is not safe enough, put half the money in a unit trust.

Currency spread

The average British company earns 30 per cent of its profits
from overseas, either by exporting, or by supplying goods
to companies that are exporting, or by owning companies
or factories based overseas. Anyone investing in British
shares has to work very hard to avoid having any exposure
to foreign currencies at all. In fact, a certain amount of
interest in foreign currencies is a good thing because for
most British people, sterling is the only currency in which
any savings are ever made. Bank deposits, equity in the
family house, everything that is realisable into cash is
valued in pounds sterling rather than in a foreign currency.
So it can be helpful to redress the balance a little.

But how far should one go? Before any decision is made on which shares to choose, the investor must decide which currencies are likely to go up in value, and which are likely to go down. The most important of these is, obviously, sterling. If it is likely to be strong, avoid shares in companies with a strong overseas content. Companies that are solely British based, such as retailers, are likely to do well, and so are companies that make their money importing things into Britain. If sterling is likely to be weak, then companies with a strong overseas content are the ones to go for, and possibly even shares on overseas stock markets (see Chapter 5).

It is necessary however, to make decisions that go beyond sterling. In 1985 and 1986, for instance, the dollar was spectacularly weak, the yen and the deutschmark were spectacularly strong. Your portfolio should mirror your future expectation on currencies, enough to match the degree of risk you want to bear, but not so much that if your judgement is wrong you have to swallow an unbearable level of loss.

Industry split

Few companies operate in just one industry, so maintaining a check on this is not as easy as it might at first sound. Make sure that you are not over-exposed in one industry, and that you are not over-exposed in interlinking businesses. The biggest customer for the mechanical engineering industry is the motor trade, for instance, so to add an engineering share to a portfolio that already contains a garage share is increasing the level of industry risk (and reward). There is nothing wrong in doing this, provided you are aware of it and what the consequences might be if the worst happens.

Frequency of change

Sometimes an investment will come along that, if it is going to be right, will be right within a fortnight or a month. Such as buying a share because you suspect a takeover might be announced shortly, or profit figures are due which the stock market expects to be bad, but you suspect will be good. Investments such as these are well and good, but they do take a great deal of monitoring. If you do not have the time to watch your shares on a daily basis, *do not get involved with them.* In any case, to have too many of these in a portfolio is a sure way to lose money. No-one can trade consistently on this basis and be right often enough to outweigh the dealing costs generated. Though doubtless your stockbroker will be pleased at the extra commissions you are generating!

There are some investments that might take two or three years to come right. Your time horizon might be a long one, but in these cases you should ask yourself whether the money might not be put to better use for a year or so until the expected event gets a little closer.

Overall, decide how long you are going to give your shares before they start earning their keep, and what your own personal time horizons are. If you expect a raging bull market to burn itself out inside a year, or have an elderly car that will need changing before too long, keep to a fairly short-term timetable. If the time you can devote to investment is limited, plan on holding shares for eighteen months or two years on average, to limit the amount of work put into managing the portfolio. Look forward and try and imagine events as they will be at a precise time in the future and ask yourself whether the share (or shares) will be right for you to hold that far ahead.

Rights issues

It is all very well for politicians to say that raising fresh money for industry is the justification for having a national stock market, but it plays the very devil with the structure of a portfolio. It also necessitates a lot of extra work, making simple but tedious calculations, selling shares to raise enough money to pay for the new rights (or selling the rights themselves), or accepting that the portfolio is going to become top-heavy in one particular share – as well as you having to find the cash to take up the extra entitlement.

To avoid rights issues, choose companies where the

balance sheets are not only cash rich but have an improving, rather than a deteriorating, cash balance. And do steer clear of some industries where the companies are notoriously rights issue prone, in particular, the banking and insurance sectors.

Other points to watch

Having established the aims of your portfolio, you will hopefully be able to start investing with the expectation of an above average degree of success. But, to stay successful, it is necessary to remember some further points.

Your objectives

After half a dozen deals, it is all too easy for the portfolio to bear little relation to the shape it started out with. Every so often go back to basics and ask yourself whether the shares in your portfolio really fit what you started out trying to achieve – remember your objectives.

Has the share done what you wanted it to?

As a share rises it is all too easy to get carried away and become hypnotised into the belief that it will go on rising forever. Everyone likes to believe they have discovered the next Polly Peck. If you buy a share having calculated that it is worth double its purchase price, however, and the share then doubles, you ought to have a pretty good reason for carrying on holding it. It may just be that the chart pattern looks good – shares that fall are usually the best ones to sell, rather than the shares that are rising, and private investors have a great advantage over the professional fund managers in that they can always sell their entire holding in a share at a moment's notice. But very, very few shares carry on rising consistently. And there comes a time to sell for everything. Do not get too emotionally attached to the company's management or its products. Selling shares is not any indication of disloyalty to Fred Bloggs down the road who happens to be finance director, it is a fact of cold realism and the performance of your investment portfolio.

Cut your losses

So, you really believe you never make a mistake? Some of the shares in your portfolio will go down, or at best stay still while the rest of the stock market goes up. Even the best of investors, at the top of their form, only get eight out of ten investment decisions right. Six out of ten right decisions is counted by professionals as a respectable figure and one which you can be proud of. So what makes you think you are perfect?

Of course, we all like to think we are different, and it hurts when one of your favourites starts heading downhill. Overcome the emotional entanglement and throw it out. Sadly, shares that start going down often continue going down. What it means is that someone out there doing the selling knows more about what is going on in that company than you do. You have to know what the other fellow is thinking, and that he has got it wrong, before you consider carrying on.

Never, never, never average your investment by buying more shares, either when they are going down, or when they are going up. Try and avoid 'selling half and keeping half' as well. This will only lead to you having a messy portfolio with more shares than you can usefully manage, and it makes for mediocre performance.

Wishing you a profitable investment

One point it would be a great shame to lose sight of, however, is that investing should be fun. Investment is, after all, only possible for those with spare money, and money should be used to increase life's pleasures and reduce its burdens, not the opposite. If investment becomes a chore rather than one of life's delights, give it up. Put the money in a unit trust, or sell the shares in your portfolio and go and spend the cash.

If you have reached the end of this book, then quite likely something other than a pure desire to get rich quickly is driving you. Perhaps it is curiosity about the issue of shares in British Gas. Perhaps the company you work for has a share quote. Perhaps you have always wanted to invest, but have only just got round to it. Fine, indulge yourself. But do not expect to always win; some, perhaps many, of the shares you choose will go down. That is inevitable, because investment is a game of probabilities. Learn from your mistakes, and swing the odds in your favour next time round.

At the back of this book we list further sources of reading which will be of interest and use to the reader. As market terms sound peculiar at the best of times (bed and breakfast is not a service offered by a hotel!), we have listed a comprehensive collection of usual and unusual terms with their definition.

If your only aim in investing on the stock market is to make a lot of money quickly, think very carefully before parting with your money. People *do* get rich quick on the stock market, but not many of them. If you have a deep thirst for wealth, you may be better off starting your own business rather than handing over cash backing a company run by someone else.

Think before you act, and research carefully before taking any investment decisions. Make sure you know more than the next investor; if you follow these rules then you should make money. If this book has played even a small part in helping you do this, then it will have served its purpose.

GLOSSARY OF TERMS

Account The period of time into which the Stock Exchange dealings are divided.

Account day The final day for dealings in Stock Exchange account. Dealings after 3.30 p.m. on that day are put forward into the new account.

Alpha A category of company that meets the very highest Stock Exchange standards, where brokers and marketmakers have to meet onerous requirements, including the reporting of all transactions within minutes of their taking place.

Allotment letter Official notification of the exact number of stocks or shares under public issue which have been allocated to the recipient.

Agency cross When a broker has matched buying and selling orders in the same share.

Arbitrage Taking advantage of price differences on particular securities on two or more markets – buying on one while at the same time selling on the other.

Assets Possessions such as stocks and shares which can be priced or valued.

Backwardation When two marketmakers' prices are so far apart that an immediate profit can be made by buying from one marketmaker and selling to another.

Bear An individual who sells shares he does not own, or does not want to deliver, and who hopes to repurchase them at a lower price, giving a profit before the delivery date becomes due. A bear market is one in which prices are going down.

Bearer stock Securities, usually European, not recorded on registers. They are physically passed by hand from seller to buyer.

Bed and breakfast Selling shares at the close of one day's business and buying them back at the start of the next for CGT purposes. The broker makes an unofficial agreement with the marketmaker in order to keep the difference between buying and selling prices to a minimum. A once common occurrence at the end of the financial year.

Beta Second highest category of listed shares. Marketmakers are obliged to deal at prices displayed on SEAQ VDU screens, and there is no 'ticker tape' of trades.

Bid price A price at which a marketmaker is willing to pay for stocks or shares. When a share is quoted as a 'bid' it generally means that there are more buyers than sellers.

Blue chip A stock market term associated with large, well-established and prosperous companies.

Bonds There are many different types of bonds but usually the word refers to fixed interest bonds issued by governments and other borrowers (also Euro Bonds). Generally these are in bearer form. Interest can be collected by detaching the coupon and sending it off to the borrower.

Book value The value at which assets appear on a balance sheet.

Bull An individual who buys shares in the hope that the price will rise before he has to pay for them.

Bull market A rising market.

Bullion Bars of specified weight of refined precious metal, gold, silver or platinum.

Capital distribution Different to a dividend in that it is a special payment to reduce company capital.

Capital gain An increase in capital value, usually cemented by a sale, in stocks and shares.

Capitalisation issue See **Scrip issue**.

Carat A unit of definition for precious metals of true product weight, pure gold is 24 carats.

Cash and new Sale of shares at the end of an old account, and their purchase back at the beginning of the new, with the agreement of the market-maker.

Cash bonus An additional payment over and above the dividend which is paid to investors when a company has made exceptional profits.

Cash settlement Payment that must be made for any transactions on the day after dealing.

Certificate of deposit A certificate which represents a transferable deposit and should be handed over when the security is sold. These documents should be kept in a secure safe place.

Charting Predicting share price movements by analysis of past price movements (see also technical analysis).

Choice price Where the best buying and selling prices offered by competing market-makers are the same, i.e. the turn is zero.

Close price The difference between bid and offer prices, usually denoting a small difference or spread between the two values.

Closing prices The price ruling at the official daily close of the Stock Exchange. If business is conducted after that time, the prices are said to be the result of 'after-hours' trading.

Common stocks A North American term used to describe equity or ordinary shares, sometimes of no par value.

Convertible loan stock A loan stock that can be converted into ordinary shares at a certain share price, between certain dates.

Coupon A slip attached to bearer securities that entitles the holder to a dividend. In order to collect interest these slips should be detached and presented to the bearers' agents. This system is very rare in Britain.

Cum When this term is used with the price of a security it means that the security comes 'with' declared divided or scrip or rights issue, etc.

Cycle A word used to describe a recurring pattern, either in an industry's trading, or in a share price.

Dealing The buying or selling of stocks and shares.

Deed of transfer The official right given to registrars of securities to transfer the deeds from one holder to another.

Delta Fourth and bottom tier of stocks quoted on the main and USM markets. These stocks trade so infrequently that their prices are not displayed on SEAQ VDU screens.

Difference The amount due from or owed to an investor at the end of a stock exchange account.

Discount The amount under its book or par value at which an asset is priced. The sum by which a coin is priced below the value of its metal content.

Discretionary account An account where the broker or agent makes investment decisions on behalf of his client(s).

Dividend The payment made by companies to their shareholders. The dividend warrant is sent along with a counterfoil which gives the shareholder exact details including the rate and amount of tax credited or deducted.

Drawings The selection of bonds for repayment under a sinking fund or the redemption of other investments by instalments.

Equity Another word for ordinary shares.

Ex When this word is noted alongside a price it means that it is after any declared event, such as a dividend payment, scrip issue, or rights issue.

Excess shares Any remaining shares after a rights issue has been taken up. The remainder may be sold on a pro rata basis in the market.

Exercise price The striking price at which a holder of a call option may buy an asset. A put option holder may also enforce a sale.

Exercise value The amount by which the striking price is below the underlying investment of a call option: the reverse is true for a put option.

Face value The legal tender value of any security. The amount due to a lender when a bond, bill or note reaches maturity.

Fixed interest security An investment over a specified period of time which yields a fixed amount of interest each year.

Flat yield Annual return on an investment at the current price.

Franked investment income Dividends sent by one company to another. These dividends have already paid corporation tax and are therefore not liable to a further tax assessment.

Forward contract An agreement for delivery of an asset at a future date and at a specified price.

Fundamental analysis The study of the factors influencing a company's profits and prospects taken in isolation and uninfluenced by share price movements.

Gamma Third tier of companies on the main and USM stock markets. Prices on SEAQ VDU screens are 'indicative only'. This means they are not binding on the marketmaker, who will be entitled to change his mind if your broker asks him to deal.

Gearing Total debt expressed as a percentage of shareholders' funds. (US term leverage.)

Gilt-edged stock A term used to describe UK Government or other similar securities.

Hard currency Currencies that have suffered only minor monetary inflation, are freely traded, and expected to retain their value.

Hedge An investment purchased at the same time as another investment in order to counter any loss it may make.

Income bonds A security that is geared to produce a high yield and to have a relatively static asset value.

Institution A professional investment body such as a pension fund, insurance company, etc.

Interim dividend The part of the annual dividend that is paid at approximately the time the half-year figures are issued.

Inter-bank rates The rate of interest which applies to transactions between banks.

In-the-money When the striking price of a call option is less than the price of the underlying investment, giving the option a theoretical real value. The reverse for a put option.

Irredeemables Fixed interest investments which have no fixed redemption date.

Issue price The value of a share on the date that it was issued.

Jobber This is the old fashioned term for a dealer on the Stock Exchange permitted to buy and sell to fellow exchange members (brokers) and through them to the public but not permitted to deal with the public directly. After the Big Bang this term was superseded by the term 'marketmakers'.

Kaffirs South African gold mining shares.

Licensed dealer A dealer in securities who is licensed to trade by the Department of Trade or by virtue of membership of a body exempted by the DTI from its regulations, such as NASDIM. They are not members of the Stock Exchange.

Limit Upper limit of purchase or sale price.

Limited market Shortage of a security which could present a difficulty when either buying or selling.

Liquidity The extent to which assets can be quickly turned into cash.

Loan stock Fixed interest security issued by a company.

London parity The sterling equivalent of an overseas stock price.

Long A bull position. A person who holds a large amount of a particular security.

Longs Government securities with redemption dates of over fifteen years. *Shorts* are securities due for repayment within five years.

Margin A percentage of the total value of an asset which has to be paid up front. Far more common in the US than in the UK. If there is an adverse fluctuation in the price then a call for more money, or *margin call*, will be made.

Make-up prices A fixing of prices by the Stock Exchange Council in order to facilitate settlement at the end of an account period.

Marketmaker Firm that specialises in making a price in securities so that other brokers can trade.

Marking names Authorised by the Bank of England to hold overseas securities on behalf of UK residents.

Marrying When a broker simultaneously links a buying and a selling order. (See **Agency cross**.)

Money stock A short-dated security which is due for repayment in the immediate future.

Name ticket A form which gives registration details of a securities purchase.

Net asset value The total amount of a company's assets which exceeds all its liabilities. The NAV rate is achieved by finding the difference between the assets and the liabilities and dividing that figure by the number of equity shares in issue.

New time The purchase of shares in one account period which will be paid for in the following account period.

Nil paid Price of the right to buy a share before the capital sum has to be put up, most usually found in a rights issue (nil paid rights).

Nominal value Face value as opposed to market value. (See also **Par value**.)

Offer The price at which sellers are offering their shares to buyers. Opposite of *Bid*. Also used in the term '*Bid and Offer spread*'.

Official List A Stock Exchange publication which gives all listed securities, along with all relevant details.

Opening price The official price of shares on the daily opening of the Stock Exchange.

Options The right of an investor to buy or to sell options on securities (including commodities) for a specified price at a specified future date. *Call options* are the right of a purchaser to buy options, and *put options* are the right of a holder to sell options. *Double options* exist when the individual can either buy or sell; *traded options* are used when the actual trading contract, or parts of its content, can be bought or sold as another option.

OTC 'Over-The-Counter Market', a market in shares conducted outside the traditional Stock Exchange, usually in shares too risky to qualify for a Stock Exchange quotation.

Out-of-the-money When the exercise price of an option is above the current share price, giving the option a theoretical value of zero.

Over-subscribed When there are more applications for an offer on a new issue of shares than there are shares available.

Par value The face value of a security or currency. This bears no relationship whatsoever to the price at which it is traded.

P/E ratio (price/earnings) Share price divided by earnings per share. The most popular form of measurement of the relative worth of various shares. The higher the figure, the more expensive the shares are.

Portfolio The division of an individual's or fund manager's assets into different types of investments for different yields and risk levels, and over differing periods of time.

Preference shares These hold the first entitlement to any dividend paid by a company and payment is made to holders *before* any payment is

185

made to the holders of ordinary (equity) shares. They usually pay a fixed annual dividend.

Premium An amount over the standard price or striking price of a security.

Prime rate A North American term indicating the best possible price for a quoted interest rate on loans by commercial banks to their clients. The US equivalent of 'bank rate' or 'base rate'.

Principal (trading as) Where a broker/marketmaker takes a position in a transaction, buying the shares for its own account that you are selling through it or vice-versa.

Prior charges The order of interest and dividend payments to debentures, loan stock, preference or equity shares.

Put-through Arrangement where a broker matches large buy and sell orders with the connivance of a marketmaker. Now more usually called an **Agency cross.**

Quotation The price made by marketmakers.

Redemption date The date when stocks are repayable.

Redemption yield Annual return on a stock plus the flat yield which accrues on a fixed interest stock at a price below its redemption rate.

Rights issue The issue of new shares to existing shareholders at a price generally lower than the current market price of its share. The offer per shareholder is based on the number of existing shares held.

Scrip issue The issue of new shares given free to existing shareholders in proportion to their existing holding.

SEAQ Stock Exchange system giving real-time bid and offer prices of competing marketmakers.

Settlement The payment made for shares either for cash or at the end of an account period.

Settlement day The day payment is due to take place for an account period.

Short When an individual has sold shares he does not own.

Stag An individual who buys new issues speculating that the value of his holding will increase over a short time period.

Stamp duty A Government tax payable on all Stock Exchange transactions, reduced from 1 per cent to 0.5 per cent.

Stop/loss order An instruction given by an investor to a broker to sell his shares should the market move adversely to his position. (Also **Stop/profit order**.)

Striking price A price at which a call option holder may buy an asset or a put option holder may enforce a sale.

Suspension When a company's shares are no longer traded on the Stock Market because of a sensitive position, either a possible take-over, liquidation or accounting irregularities.

Takeover The purchase of one company by another.

Talisman A simplified transfer system of computerised accounts for most UK-listed company securities.

Tap stock A Government stock on offer which is not fully subscribed.

Technical analysis A system whereby price movements are analysed in connection with supply and demand over a specified period of time.

Tender Shares or Government stocks, offered for subscription with a fixed minimum, but no maximum, price. The buyer decides the price that he or she wants to pay, and 'tenders' at this amount.

Third market A market run by the Stock Exchange in the shares of companies that do not meet the listing requirements of either the main or USM markets.

Time deposit A deposit that cannot be withdrawn until a fixed date.

Touch The best buying and best selling prices after consulting all marketmakers.

Treasury securities Government notes of obligatory debts which take the form of bills, notes or bonds.

Transfer deed This verifies the transfer of securities from seller to buyer.

Turn Difference between buying and selling prices (see **Backwardation**).

Unassented bonds Variation in the original bond contract terms where the change has not been agreed by the holders.

Undated securities Stocks which have no fixed repayment date.

Unfranked income Interest and dividends received by a company and which have not paid corporation tax.

Unlisted Securities Market Is the second tier market of quoted securities, traded on the Stock Exchange. Requirements for a USM quote are less onerous than those for a full listing.

Unquoted securities Stocks and shares which are not listed on any recognised Stock Exchange.

Warrant An instrument together with a specified amount of money enables the holder to buy ordinary shares for a fixed price at a certain time. Metal warrants are also used in the commodity markets and show proof of ownership. They are also bearer warrants.

Yankees American stocks and shares.

Yield The return on an investment via its dividend payments. A yield gap is the difference between the average yield on gilt-edged stocks and equity shares.

APPENDIX I: SOURCES OF INFORMATION

Barrons: US weekly investment newspaper, worthwhile reading for those thinking of investing directly on the US stock market. Annual subscription £116. Address: 200 Liberty Street, New York, NY 10281, USA.

The Daily Telegraph: Every weekday plus Saturdays, this paper lists stock and share prices; in addition, every Saturday there is the Family-Money-Go-Round feature. Telegraph Publications produce books on financial matters including the highly acclaimed *101 Ways of Investing and Saving Money*. A catalogue of publications is available from Telegraph Publications, Peterborough Court, At South Quay, 181 Marsh Wall, London E14 9SR.

Datastream: On-line computerised statistical and share price chart drawing service that, while probably the best single aid to investment, is possibly way out of reach of the average investor. Annual subscription from £2,000, plus line charges. Address: Monmouth House, City Road, London EC1.

The Economist: General weekly magazine devoted to spotting changes in trends worldwide, and with good financial coverage. Annual subscription £60. Address: 23a St James's Street, London SW1A 1HF.

Extel Statistical Services: Provides indexed card system on company information. This could prove to be far too expensive for most private investors but is available free of charge at many large public libraries. Alternatively, cards can be bought singly. Address: 34 Paul Street, London EC2.

Financial Weekly: Weekly investment and general business magazine. Annual subscription £47. Address: 14 Greville Street, London EC1N 8SB.

Fleet Street Letter: Fortnightly newsletter specialising in high risk, high reward, small companies. Includes free investment advice service. Annual subscription £96 (but usually has '£30 off' offer for new subscribers). Address: 3 Fleet Street, London EC4B 4SL.

Investors Chronicle: Weekly investment magazine with particularly good coverage of company results and annual reports. It also has a free service obtaining annual reports for investors. Annual subscription £52. Address: Minster House, Arthur Street, London EC4R 9AX.

Monthly Digest of Statistics: A fat monthly catalogue full of figures that show growth rates, price rate increases, spending trends and employment trends, etc., in various industries. Cost £5.75 a month. Address: Central Statistical Office, Great George Street, London SW1P 3AQ.

Seestats: A computerised share chart drawing programme that is designed for use on most popular personal computers (including the BBC, the Spectrum, and the IBM PC). It enables investors to draw charts comparing company share prices, indices, on a log or an arithmetical basis. It calculates moving averages and 'golden crosses', and the first disc comes loaded with share price data on a series of leading companies. It is possible to buy back-data, ready loaded, on a range of other companies for an extra fee. Other than that, you load the data yourself, for as many companies as you like. Cost £75 per annum. Write to: Bob Crowe, 20 Rozelle Road, Parkstone, Poole, Dorset BH1 40BX (0202-742384).

Traded Option Newsletter: As the title suggests. Annual subscription £110 a year. Address: Consort House, 26 Queensway, London W2 3RX.

USM Review: Tipsheet/magazine specialising in shares quoted on the USM market. Annual subscription £95. Address: 3 Fleet Street, London EC4Y 1AU.

USM Stock Market Handbook: A useful directory of information on individual USM shares. The same company also publishes a more expensive handbook on the full market's largest stocks. Cost £15. Address: Extel Statistical Services, 34 Paul Street, London EC2.

What Investment?: Monthly investment magazine, with an emphasis on the private investor, particularly the relative newcomer to investing. Annual subscription £25. Address: Consort House, 26 Queensway, London W2 3RX.

INDEX

Accountant, dealing through, 63, 69
Accounts
  acquisition accounting, 104;
  company, 12, 96, 102, 117, 123;
  currency changes, 111–12; merger
  accounting, 104
Acid test ratio, 122–3
Advertising/marketing sector, 159–60
All-Share Index, 100, 154
American Depository Receipts (ADR),
  78

Backwardation, 76
Bambers Stores, 17–21, 137, 139
Bank deposit accounts, 33
Bank manager, dealing through, 63
Banking sector, 160–2
Bargain, 76, 79
Big Bang, 76, 77–82
  marketmaking and broking, 80–1;
  on-screen dealing, 82; small
  companies, 82
Blue chip shares, 23
Brewing sector, 162–3
British Gas, 16, 58
British Rate and Data (BRAD), 159
British Telecom, 11, 15–16
Britoil, 22
Brokers see Stockbrokers
Building Society accounts, 33, 98
Business Expansion Scheme (BES), 26

Capital base, 161
Capital gains tax, 25, 29, 36, 63
  gilt-edged securities, 51; Personal
  Equity Plan, 43
Capital gearing ratio, 122
Capital growth sacrificed for income,
  171
Capital ratio, 161
Capitalisation issue, 104
Chart analysis, 133–58
  drawing, 152–8; moving average,
  149–50; price, 153; time, 153
Choice price, 75
Company
  accounts, 12, 96, 102, 117, 123, 162;
  acid test ratio, 122–3; analysis,

117–32; balance sheet, 117, 120–1;
  capital gearing ratio, 122;
  consolidated balance sheet, 117–18,
  123; contingent liabilities, 120;
  current ratio, 122; debts 120–1,
  126–7; fixed assets, 120, 121; income
  gearing ratio, 122; inventory
  control, 124–6; receivables/payables
  control, 126–7; reports, 12, 96,
  117–18, 162; source and application
  of funds, 123; valuing, 118, 120
Compensation schemes, 63–4
Contingent liabilities, 120
Contract note, 76, 195
Contracting sector, 163
Corporation tax, 99
Currency spread, 86–7, 171, 175–6
Current ratio, 122

Dealing, 75–7
  on-screen, 82
Dealing costs, 23, 27–8, 30, 78–9, 81–2
  divisible commission, 70–1; foreign
  investments, 90–3; gilt-edged
  securities, 51; investment trusts,
  45–6; Personal Equity Plans, 44–5;
  unit trusts, 38
Debenhams' stockbroking units, 69
Directors
  sale of shares by, 20; stockbrokers
  as, 80
Dividends, 12
  collection, 63; figures on "per
  share" basis, 101; price/earnings
  ratio, 106–9; stock market analysis,
  98–9; taxation, 98
Dixons, 17–21
Dow Jones Index, 95–6

Employment agencies, 160
Engineering sector, 164
Estate agencies, 160
Exports/overseas sales, 111–12
Extel card, 72, 103

FIMBRA, 63
Financial Times Indices, 100, 107–9
Fixed assets, 120, 121

Fixed interest investments, 51–60, 172
gilt-edged securities, 51–8; reverse
yield gap, 100–1
Foreign currency, 86–7, 111, 171, 175
movements, 163
Foreign investments, 83–94
dealing costs, 90–3; disadvantages,
89–90
Fraud, 74

Gearing, 112, 122
Gilt-edged loans
tax on accrued interest, 59–60
Gilt-edged securities, 51–8, 98
Consuls, 100; dealing costs, 51, 58;
Financial Times indices, 100;
high-coupon stocks, 52–3, 100;
index-linked, 58–9; interest, 52;
long-dated, 56, 100; low-coupon
stocks, 53–4, 57, 100;
medium-coupon stocks, 54–5, 100;
medium-dated, 56; National
Savings Stock Register, 51; partly
paid stocks, 58; short-dated, 56;
short-term trading, 58; undated, 56;
War Loan, 52, 55, 56, 100; yields,
56–8, 100–1
Gold, investing in, 35–7

High borrowing, 20

Income Bonds, 31–2
Indexed Income Bonds, 31
Insider trading, 95–6
Insurance policies, 34–5
Insurance sector, 164–6
Interest, operational gearing, 112
Inventory, 124–6, 169
Investment
fixed interest, 51–60, 100–1, 172;
size, 26–8; strategy, 171–80
Investment trusts, 45–50
advantages, 45–6; dealing costs,
45–6; discounts, 46–7; split level,
47–9
Investor
charting actions, 133; credit checks
on, 75; future earning power, 24;
non-resident, 29, 52, 60; outgoings,
25, 28; pension lump sum, 24;
pensioners, 24, 25–6, 49;
personality, 23–4, 28; tax position,
29

Jobber *see* Marketmaker
"Junk bond" shares 41

Krugerrands, 36

Licensed Dealer in Securities, 63–4, 74
Lloyd's syndicates, 164
London & Liverpool Trust, 21–2, 137,
139

Macarthy press cutting service, 103

Marketmakers, 72, 75–6, 78, 79
and brokers, 79–81; "turn", 27–8
Mineral sector, 166–9
exploration, 167–8; production,
168–9
Mortgage as investment, 25

National Savings
Certificates, 30–1; Income Bonds,
31–2; Indexed Income Bonds, 31;
Investment Account, 32; Premium
Bonds, 32; Stock Register, 51
Newspaper stories, 20
Nil paid rights, 128–9

On-screen dealing, 82
Operational gearing, 112
Over-The-Counter Market (OTC), 26,
74
Overbought/oversold ratio, 152
Overseas based organisations, 74

Pension payments, 25–6
Additional Voluntary Contribution
(AVC), 26
Pensioners, 24, 25–6
split level investment trusts, 49
Personal Equity Plans (PEP), 11, 26,
43–5
ceiling, 43; tax advantages, 43;
voting rights, 44–5
Polly Peck, 20–1, 137, 138
Portfolio
minimum, 26, 72; spread, 174–6;
strategy, 171–80
Premium Bonds, 32
Price/earnings ratio, 106–9, 133, 161
Privatisations, 11, 15–16, 22, 58
Profit
depreciation, 113–14; influences on,
109–115; margins, 114–15;
operational gearing, 112;
overstated, 113; reports, 12, 96, 117
"Put-through", 81

Resource Technology, 137, 140
Retailers, investing in, 20
Rights issues, 12, 104, 127–31, 172,
177–8
Rises/falls ratio, 152
Risk, 24, 86–7, 171, 172, 174
Roll-up funds, 33–4, 87

Scrip issue, 104, 131–2
SEAQ, 75
Sentiment indicator, 151
Shares
"A" shares, 103; All-Share Index,
100, 154; alternatives to, 29–50;
analysis, 95–132; annual rate of
increase, 21; assets per share, 104,
105–6; authorised, 102; "B" shares,
103; blue chip, 23; capital gains tax,
25; capitalisation issue, 104, 131–2;
collapse, 23–6; dealing costs, 23,

Shares – *cont.*
27–8, 30; deferred, 102–3; drop in value, 17; earnings per share, 104–5; Executive share option schemes, 103; foreign companies quoted in London, 87–9; FT Industrial Index, 100; heavy, 132; income, 171, 172; institution purchasing, 146; issued, 102; "junk bond", 41; moving average, 149–50; numbers issued, 101–6; ordinary, 102, 103; over-priced, 132; participating, 103; preference, 102, 105; price charts, 133–58; price/earnings ratio, 106–9, 133; restricted, 103; reverse yield gap, 100–1; rights issues, 104, 127–31, 172, 177–8; risk/reward ratio, 172, 174; sale by directors, 20; scrip issue, 104, 131–2; selling, 20–1, 178–9; shareholders' funds, 117–18, 120, 121; speculative, 23; spread, 174–5; takeover bids, 103, 171; USM, 44, 68; yield, 172
Solicitor, dealing through, 63
Stamp duty, 27
foreign investments, 90–3; gilt-edged securities, 51; unit trusts, 38
Stock Exchange
account system, 76; compensation fund, 63; divisible commission, 70–1; foreign, 78, 87; London, 70, 78, 81, 87; membership, 77; regional, 70; share price system (SEAQ), 75
Stock market
advance/decline ratio, 151–2; analysis, 95–116; movements, 150–1; sentiment indicator, 151
Stock turn, 20, 124–6
Stockbrokers, 12, 20, 63, 78, 80
advertising by, 64; annual reports, 72; bulletins, 69; choosing, 64–74; client credit checks, 75; commission, 27, 38, 51, 59, 70–1, 78–9, 81–2, 90–3; dealing directly with, 63; as directors, 80; Extel card, 72, 103; London, 26, 27; marketmaking, 72,

79–81; minimum portfolio, 26, 72; mixed capacity, 79–81; private investor, 69, 81; protected payment structure, 16; research, 66–7, 72, 79, 81, 90; retail units, 69; size of firm, 64, 66, 72; special roles, 69–70; Stock Exchange compensation fund, 63; unit trust management, 67–8
Stocks
convertible loan, 41, 131; conversion into ordinary shares, 102; gilt-edged *see* Gilt-edged securities; loan, 59; Over-The-Counter (OTC), 26, 74

Takeover
bid, 171; in exchange for share issue, 103
Tax, 29, 33
capital gains, 25, 29, 36, 43, 51, 63; corporation, 99; dividends, 98; foreign investments, 87, 89, 90–3; gilt-edged loans, 59–60; impact on company profits, 116; income, 43; mortgage interest relief, 25; National Savings, 30–2; non-resident status, 29, 52, 60; pension schemes, 35; relief, 25–6, 35; split level investment trusts, 49; stamp duty, 27, 38, 51; transfer stamp, 27; value added, 36, 37
Textile sector, 170
Trading, 63–82
insider, 95–6; through intermediary, 63–4; through stockbroker *see* Stockbrokers
Transfer stamp, 27
"Turn", 27–8

Unit trusts, 24, 26, 37–43, 67–8
advantages, 37; choosing, 38, 40; dealing costs, 38; investment trusts compared, 46; size of fund, 41
USM shares, 44, 68

Value added tax, 36, 37

War Loan, 52, 55, 56, 100

Yield curve, 56–8